THE
X-FACTOR
SWING

AND OTHER SECRETS
TO POWER AND DISTANCE

THE
X-FACTOR
SWING

AND OTHER SECRETS
TO POWER AND DISTANCE

JIM McLEAN

WITH JOHN ANDRISANI

HarperCollins*Publishers*

HarperCollins books may be purchased for educational, business, or sales promotional use. For information, please write to: Special Markets Department, HarperCollins Publishers, Inc., 10 East 53rd Street, New York, New York 10022.

FIRST EDITION

ISBN 0–06–270142–8

Designed by Jessica Shatan

Library of Congress Cataloging-in-Publication Data

McLean, Jim.
    The X-factor swing : and other secrets to power and distance / by Jim McLean with John Andrisani. — 1st ed.
      p.   cm.
    ISBN 0-06-270142-8
    1. Swing (Golf)   I. Andrisani, John.   II. Title.
GV979.S9M33 1996   96-43829
796.352'3—dc20

01 ❖/RRD 10 9 8 7

To Justine, Matt, and Jon

CONTENTS

ACKNOWLEDGMENTS   VII

FOREWORD   IX

INTRODUCTION   XIII

PART I: POWER FUNDAMENTALS

Is Golf Different from Other Sports?   3

Right-sided Golf Versus Left-sided Golf: What's Right?   4

What's Feel and What's Real?   6

One or Two Pivot Points?   9

The Law of the Athletic Throw   11

Basic Pivot Actions and the Natural Throwing Motion   12

First Things First   14

Analyzing the Throwing Motion   16

The Body Press   18

Moving Center: On the Backswing   20

Mclean's Power Leaks: On the Backswing   22

Moving Center: On the Downswing   24

Correct Head Movement: On the Downswing   27

Looking Off the Ball   29

To Lift or Not to Lift   33

Seeing Is Believing   38

Power Components   39

Assembling the Engine   42

The Power Coil: Breaking It Down   44

Returning to Impact   47

What You Must Know   50

More on Hogan   52

Throwing Principles   53

Effortless Power Versus Powerless Effort   55

Vital Upper Left Arm Movements   57

The Vital Left Wrist Position   58

Quick Tips for Generating High Clubhead Speed   59

The Hips Rise   60

PART II: THE X-FACTOR

The X-Factor: A Preview   65
The X-Factor Set: Body Positioning   69
The X-Factor Backswing: Creating the "Gap"   72
Backswing Drills: For Creating the "Gap"   78
Backswing Problems   79
Backswing Corrections   83
Great Backswing Images   85
The X-Factor Downswing: Closing the "Gap"   86
Downswing Drills: For Closing the "Gap"   93
Good Player's Disease: The Downswing Right Shoulder Drop   95
Correct Body Actions for a Controlled Draw/Controlled Fade   97
Tour Player Analysis: Profile of a Lesson Program   98
Final Review: Load, Unload, Explode   108

ACKNOWLEDGMENTS

Mike McTeigue, founder and CEO of SportSense, worked with me at Doral to test the PGA Tour players. With the information Mike collected from the SportSense computer, I wrote the first X-Factor article for <u>GOLF</u> M*agazine* in 1992. After that, wherever I went to speak for the PGA of America, the X-Factor was topic number one. Everybody wanted to hear more about it.

Mike McTeigue's company uses real-time motion to analyze golf swings and audio feedback to help train golfers. It's a phenomenal way to gain valuable research data, and many golfers improve very quickly using SportSense.

Prior to those tests, I had been teaching and speaking about the Four Turns in the golf swing—an entirely new concept. The information I gained through the use of Mike's computer confirmed many things I had observed (and also read), but had never been able to prove.

I thank the staff at the Doral Learning Center (which consists of seventeen PGA Professionals). I regularly discussed the book's content with them, and asked them to challenge every profound point or statement, as a means of testing its credibility. Their insightful and highly valued operations are much appreciated.

I also thank my cowriter, John Andrisani, who not only served as an expert sounding board, but added to the book's creativity. In fact, he named the X-Factor when it first appeared in <u>GOLF</u> M*agazine*.

I owe great gratitude to the photographers, Leonard Kamsler and Keiichi Sato, for their fine work.

Also, I thank artist Jim McQueen, who did a superb job of conveying the X-Factor instructional message.

FOREWORD

Many golfers who meet me are envious of my job. They think that because I'm the senior instruction editor of <u>GOLF</u> M*agazine*, I get to play the greatest courses in the world, with the greatest players in the world. They also think that I receive regular lessons from the greatest teachers in the world. Consequently, in their minds, I must be a scratch golfer.

To be honest, ever since joining <u>GOLF</u> M*agazine* in October 1982, I've enjoyed my job very much. I've also played some of the finest courses in the world, including Cypress Point in California, Ballybunion in Ireland, Shinnecock Hills in New York, and Augusta National in Georgia. I've also been lucky enough to have played with some of the top tour professionals, most notably Seve Ballesteros, Curtis Strange, and Chi Chi Rodriguez. As for my handicap, it's not scratch.

Frankly, when I joined <u>GOLF</u> M*agazine* I carried a three handicap. However, in the years that followed, my handicap rose steadily to ten. Ironically, that was because every time I picked up the phone, a teacher would provide me with a new swing theory that I just had to try. Because of this influx of free, well-meaning instruction, every time I stood on the tee, numerous swing thoughts would race through my mind. I didn't know whether to trigger the swing by bringing my left shoulder toward my chin, pushing my hands away from the ball, turning my right hip in a clockwise direction, rotating my left knee past the ball—you name it. It got to the point where I'd go through a round, trying a new tip on practically every drive and approach shot. Surely, you've had similar experiences.

Nowadays, I still try out different tips. After all, that's a big part of my job. I figure if a new swing key works for me, maybe it will work wonders for the 1.5 million golfers who subscribe to <u>GOLF.</u> I must confess, however, that I save my experimenting for the practice tee. On the course, I try to rely on one swing thought to carry me through the entire eighteen holes. My handicap has gone back down, too, so I must be on the right track.

I owe a lot of the credit for my improvement to Jim McLean, a renowned instructor who teaches top pros, and club-level golfers like me, at the Doral Golf Learning Center in Miami, Florida. One important thing that Jim has done for me is make me understand that the so-called fundamentals, such as keeping your head still on the backswing, and continuing to look at the ball until it's struck, are not really fundamentals at all. Jim teaches what he calls the "new fundamentals"—basic positions of the setup and swing that are common to the majority of PGA Tour pros who make their living playing golf. As Jim says, "The basics that many teachers rely on at their schools do little more than create a nation of slicers. That's because they are outdated tips that were used long ago, when golfers played with hickory-shafted clubs. I prefer to teach fundamentals that are shared by pros who make a habit of shooting scores under seventy, not just barely under one hundred."

What's so good about Jim is that he didn't just pick these new fundamentals out of the blue. There's no smoke and mirrors with Jim. If he tells you a golf secret, it's one he's learned from talking to the pros or watching them swing on film. In fact, that was the case with the discovery of the X-Factor.

After going on the road for a few years to study the world's most talented players, Jim noticed something that disproved the theory that a golfer has to turn his hips and shoulders to the max in order to generate power. Because this advice is given to many of the 28 million golfers around the world, on practically a daily basis, Jim figured he'd better do some further research.

To shorten a long story, Jim and fellow pro, Mike McTeigue, tested a number of pros, using a highly sophisticated device called a SportSense Swing Motion Trainer. What Jim observed proved to be true. Thus the X-Factor was born.

In December 1992, GOLF Magazine revealed the secret of the X-Factor backswing in a cover story that turned out to be an all-time best-seller. A year later, another blockbuster cover story, "X-Factor 2," taught golfers how to release the powerful energy they create on the backswing.

From that point in time to the present, McLean has done further studies on the X-Factor, learning even more about it. What's more, he's made some other new discoveries, involving critical movements of the swing, such as determining the efficient pivoting action that allows the pros to hit the ball so far and straight.

My advice is not to turn to the pages in this book explaining the X-Factor until you've read about Jim's other swing secrets, involving body motion and vital club positions, which he discovered while working with pros in his scientific-looking teaching studio at Doral. Only then will you be able to clearly understand the X-Factor movement and incorporate it into your own swing. Be prepared, however. These swing keys are very different from those you've been given by your local pro or playing partner. In fact, Jim's advice is likely to be the exact opposite of what you've been taught. The only difference is, it works!

JOHN ANDRISANI
Orlando, Florida

INTRODUCTION

BEGINNING

Golfers and instruction books focus most of their attention on the swing of the club. When I teach at any level, I always break the golf swing into two basic components:

1. What is the golf club doing?
2. What is the body doing?

I believe that the two interrelate. I'm not sure which is more important; I do know that each component dramatically affects the other.

This book will focus on body action. I will detail critical body positions and body angles and show you how to get into the positions of the best ball strikers.

EDUCATION

I began working at private clubs in 1975. I was one of the six teaching professionals at Westchester Country Club, which is still the site of the Buick Classic. At Westchester we had 1,800 members, 45 holes of golf, a great hotel, and a huge practice range. I was privileged to teach with experienced and well-respected teachers, including the famous "Lighthorse" Harry Cooper (winner of 26 tour events) and Mary Lena Faulk (one of the professionals chosen by Harvey Penick to write the introduction to his *Little Red Book*).

Mary Lena and I were responsible for the ladies' clinics, which became very successful. We had 120 women participating. I also ran a very large junior program with Bob and Craig Watson. (Bob was another Harvey Penick protégé and the Director of Golf at Westchester.)

Having been solely a player until then, I had a lot to learn. However, it would have been difficult to find a better place to start. I worked five summers at Westchester, and spent the winters working very hard on my teaching and playing skills with people like Ken Venturi, Gardner Dickinson, Jackie Burke, Joe Nichols, Jimmy Ballard, Claude Harmon, Tony Penna, and Bob Toski.

I also visited various golf schools to watch reputable instructors teach. I quickly saw that some teachers were a whole lot better than others. It was no contest. I saw that to be a great teacher required that you get results. It wasn't always the smartest teachers who succeeded. In fact, some highly intelligent instructors were very poor at helping players improve.

Since then, I've always told my staff at Doral, and our other academies, that although we have great locations, championship golf courses, high-tech learning centers, the best range balls, terrific personal playing skills, a great understanding of the golf swing, and beautifully coordinated matching outfits—we are only good if we help students improve. It's as simple as that.

In the late 1970s, I came up with the concept of dividing golf into four distinct, but separate, areas. Seeing that one secret to great coaching in all sports was a step-by-step building block approach, I began doing the same in golf. Coming up with the 25% Theory, I divided the game of golf into the Long Game, the Short Game, the Mental Game, and the Management Game. I gave equal weight to each distinct area. In the early 1980s, I spoke about the 25% Theory at PGA education seminars; and in the mid-1980s, at National PGA workshops. It was a great way to look at golf and I still use this concept today. It's gratifying to see that many other instructors now use this concept as the basis for their teaching.

Since then, I've looked at each of the major areas and subdivided them. Of course, the Short Game is easily divided into subgames, such as putting, chipping, pitching, and bunker play. For the Long Game, I began to look at the golf swing containing two major components: the *body* and the *club*. I began to look closely at isolating each one from the other. This book is the culmination of my research on the body action and body sequencing in the golf swing. By isolating, we clear things up. We put parts of the swing under the microscope. We shine a light on misconceptions. Either you're doing it or you're not.

I would like this book to fall under the same microscope. If you read this book and then understand what you must do to achieve balance, power, and simplicity in your golf swing—and then you actually do it—this will be a successful book.

John Andrisani and I have laid out this book in the short-chapter form. Each segment of the book has clarity and can easily be found again for your review. One thing is for sure, good teaching is precise and crystal clear.

Back to my education. In 1979, I became the head professional at the prestigious Sunningdale Country Club in Scarsdale, New York. In 1983, I moved to the head job at Quaker Ridge, which had the number one ranked golf course in the metropolitan section. It was a fabulous job that helped me get a position as the winter director of golf at Tamarisk (in Palm Springs, California) in 1987–88. Then, in 1988, Jim Hand (past president of the United States Golf Association) flew out to California to offer me the director of golf position at Sleepy Hollow Country Club (Scarborough on the Hudson, New York). I felt that this was probably the number one job in the metropolitan section because of the great membership, the huge facility—including 27 holes of golf, horse stables, 18 miles of riding trails, tennis, and swimming. "Sleepy" even hosted a Senior PGA Tour event. It was a job I couldn't turn down.

At all the clubs I worked at, I built video rooms or small learning centers. At Sleepy Hollow, they actually built an entire new range, complete with a Learning Center for me. It was perfect. You could walk right out of the center directly onto the range. No wasted time.

Back then, many tour players came to Sleepy Hollow to work on their game. I had the best video equipment and super-talented assistants, three who later became Top 100–ranked teachers in America. Some of the pros using our Learning Center included Tom Kite, Hal Sutton, Brad Faxon, Peter Jacobsen, Mark McCumber, Lennie Clements, Debra Vidal, Lauri Merten, Gary Player, Jim Dent, Al Geiberger, and many more.

I also taught most of the top-rated junior boys and girls, the top-rated men and women, and the top-rated seniors in the metropolitan area. Of course, my main focus was the full lesson program at Sleepy Hollow. We had a lot of fine players, and over ninety children in our junior program. So the Sleepy Hollow Learning Center was like Grand Central Station. We stayed incredibly busy with players of every caliber, and I continued to collect valuable research data.

When I took the director of instruction position at Doral in 1991, I inherited Jimmy Ballard's Learning Center. The owners of Doral, the Kaskel family, were big golfers and had great appreciation for the game. They always had fine teachers at Doral and they felt that, over the 30 years of Doral's existence, top teaching was a big asset.

At first I only worked the winter months, then returned to Sleepy Hollow for the summer. However, by 1993, I knew I would have to move to Doral. The golf school business had exploded, and the growth opportunities were unlimited. Plus a new corporation (KSL) had purchased Doral and promised to upgrade all facilities. So, despite the fact that my family and I loved Sleepy Hollow, we moved to Miami. My focus was now 100 percent teaching.

Research

Early on in my life I worked with good instructors, played extensive competitive golf, and had the opportunity to play with top tour players. I was always interested in what they thought about the swing. I usually took notes, plus tape-recorded or videotaped these sessions. It was a good way to collect data from expert sources. At Sleepy Hollow we began to videotape every player during the Senior PGA Tour event and analyze every swing. Later, when I took over Doral, we videotaped every player every year during the Doral Ryder Open, and carefully analyzed every swing.

This research is different from sitting in an office and figuring out the perfect model according to physics and geometry. Although geometry and physics are important, the office I used was the real world, and golf's greatest players. I learned this detailed research system from Carl Welty, one of the best golf research experts in the world. Since the 1960s, Carl has filmed or taped PGA Tour players swinging. He always compared the best players against all those who didn't make it. In the late 1960s, we began to work together. As time went on, and I traveled around the world, I would feed Carl ideas and concepts to check out against his vast library. Eventually, we made a tape that consisted of players who had won at least two major championships, figuring this was one good test. What did they do that was somewhat similar? Were there any similarities? Did they do things that the also-rans did not do? What were those differences? Some of the answers can be found inside this book, such as how different golfers look on the backswing and how similar they look at impact.

Synopsis

This book will tell you some of the secrets I've learned from many years of studying the best, playing with the best, and teaching the best. In this book I've confined almost all of my attention to body actions, because it is here that you will see the greatest similarities.

If you can master some of the moves, some of the body positions, and some of the key body angles described in these pages, I know you will improve your balance and your golf swing. You'll be more consistent, and you'll hit the ball longer—perhaps a lot longer. So, let's get started with the athletic moves required in golf, and the tremendous importance of correct body actions.

Jim McLean
Miami, Florida

PART I

POWER FUNDAMENTALS

IS GOLF DIFFERENT FROM OTHER SPORTS?

If you read most golf books, or listen to many past and modern-day teachers, you would have to answer this question with the affirmative.

I've heard well-known teachers at workshops around the world say that everything you do naturally at golf is absolutely dead wrong. The same teachers tell students that golf is a left-sided game, and unlike any other sport. Furthermore, the movements of the golf swing are unnatural. I say this is probably one of the chief reasons golf is so difficult for many people to learn, and why so many beginners give up the game after a few lessons. You see, golf is *not* different from most other sports, in terms of the basic body movements involved. It is remarkably similar to the throwing actions used by a baseball infielder, as Ben Hogan pointed out in his best-selling book, *Five Lessons*. In fact, it is similar to many other sports.

On the backswing, both the golfer and baseball infielder shift most of their weight to the right side, while the right arm flows back and folds at the elbow. On the downswing, these players shift their weight to the left side, rotate around the left leg, then fully release the right arm. In both cases, their secret to generating good power is keeping the right arm and wrist relaxed or "soft," and using the body to create a whip and a repeating action.

RIGHT-SIDED GOLF VERSUS LEFT-SIDED GOLF: WHAT'S RIGHT?

Beginning in 1976, I had the opportunity to begin extensive work with Ken Venturi. Venturi was described by his mentor Byron Nelson as the finest iron player in the history of golf. That was quite a strong statement when you consider that Nelson is recognized as one of the all-time great players.

One of the first things I learned from Ken was that he relied heavily on the right side. Much of what he learned from years of personal work with Byron Nelson, and the countless practice and competitive rounds with Ben Hogan, focused on the right arm and right side of the body. Venturi is indeed a right-sided player. Since then, I've learned that many great players focus more on the right half of the body. The old cliché "golf is a left-sided game" perhaps is not so valid after all.

In 1977, I began to visit a new type of instructor. His name was Jimmy Ballard, and he was teaching golf in a remote part of Alabama, Pell City. The thing was, Ballard was booked two months ahead. You couldn't get in to see him any sooner. Plus

I'm with Ken Venturi, one of my most influential golf swing mentors.

he didn't just give half-hour lessons: He conducted two-day golf schools. Day one focused on the backswing; day two on the forward swing. Even the many PGA club professionals and PGA Tour pros who visited Ballard had to attend a one-hour introductory class, then go through the school. No private lessons for anyone not first attending the school.

There were several unique things about the Ballard school. Every school was full with players of all levels in attendance. The cornerstone of his backswing theory was employing a lateral shift into the right side. In the late 1970s, over one hundred touring pros visited Pell City for instruction. Ballard despised words like "pull," or "turn," so he would not use them in his teaching. He was a pure *right-sided* teacher.

Almost all of what Ballard did was unprecedented. He was unorthodox in every respect, including not being a PGA member. Nearly every established instructor I spoke with thought Jimmy was crazy. The old left-sided theory would not easily die. It was an accepted part of golf truth. Only I could further confirm, even back then, that what instructors taught and what great players actually did was often quite different. Years later, I would see several of those anti-Ballard instructors using Jimmy Ballard phrases and teaching exactly what they once criticized.

WHAT'S FEEL
AND WHAT'S REAL?

Throughout the 1970s, as golf exploded in popularity, the primary axioms taught in golf were: (1) don't move; (2) stay steady; (3) turn around a fixed center; (4) make golf a left-sided game; (5) keep your right elbow close to your right side; (6) pull the butt end of the grip at the ball; (7) keep your right side passive; and (8) drive the legs. Not all teachers were in this camp. However, a huge majority were. Most golfers and instructors were in the dark ages of teaching. They were teaching the old clichés and feels that simply were not factual. As Ballard and other insightful teachers say, "Feel will fool you." In other words, what you feel you're doing is often not what you're actually doing.

Ballard, Venturi, and Welty taught me to separate feel from fact. They encouraged me to take what a top tour player said he or she did during the swing, with a grain of salt. Furthermore, they taught me to analyze a player's swing closely, ideally on videotape, and determine for myself what was actually going on. Ever since, I've been a just-the-facts kind of teacher, who never forgets Welty's words, "Don't tell me, show me." I've learned from studying thousands of hours of film, videotape, and now computer technology that it's not what they say, rather it's what they do.

Almost every golfer will feel a certain move in a slightly different way. In fact, some golfers feel exactly the same move in exactly opposite ways. One will feel it with the right side, while the other with the left side. One will feel the pull, the other the push. My job, in this book, is to actually show you what I know happens in the golf swing regarding body movements and body sequencing. The X-Factor and other swing secrets come from extensive research and extensive observation. I've determined that just about anybody can write down a plausible golf-swing theory. They may even teach a good method that fits a certain number of students. What I hope to show you are the factual fundamentals of a sound swing—not what sounds good, not what is scientifically the perfect model swing; rather what has stood the test of time—what works on the playing field under the stress of competition.

THE RIGHT ARM EXAMPLE

One thing many top PGA Tour professionals agree on is that the action of the right arm is critical to generating power in the golf swing. This action is very similar to the action used to skim a stone across the surface of a pond, or throw a ball. The right arm only works correctly and powerfully when the body is positioned properly, and moves in a certain simple sequence. By focusing attention on your right arm and right side, you will (if you are right-handed) generally improve much faster than trying to train your much less coordinated left side.

Byron Nelson has always called the right arm a "floater." By that he means the right arm is somewhat free in the takeaway. I really like this concept. It does not attach to the right side of the body early in the swing. Rather, it floats away from the body. This helps create width and leverage, and allows the right arm to become the swing's whip. If you tuck the right arm close to your body early in the backswing, you narrow your swing arc and weaken the turn of your upper torso. In short, you lose the whip—the power.

As important as the right-arm movement is on the backswing, it's the move from the top of the backswing to the beginning of the downswing that separates the top ball strikers from the average player. The sequence of motion for a throw is shift, rotate the body center, release the right arm. That's identical to the one used by top pros when swinging a golf club. That's a fact!

The action of the right arm is critical to power golf. The right arm only works correctly and powerfully when the body is positioned properly and moves in a simple sequence. Great players have always felt a sense of pull and hitting up against a braced left side. Early stop-action photography correctly showed tremendous lag in the hands and club on the downswing. When

I agree with Byron Nelson, who thinks the right arm should move away from the body, or "float," to create width in the swing.

comparing the professional against the high handicapper, the easiest observation was usually the throw from the top by the high handicapper. The obvious conclusion was that the dominant right hand took over and ruined the swing. I say that conclusion is wrong. The sense of pull on the left side comes from good body work, and not from consciously pulling the left arm or the grip of the club. Do that and you'll never reach your power potential.

ONE OR TWO PIVOT POINTS?

In teaching the golf swing, there are numerous disagreements among instructors about the various positions or movements. Possibly the most controversial topic concerns the pivot actions of the swing. Personally, I strongly believe in the two-pivot point swing. However, to be truthful, there are still many instructors who believe wholeheartedly in the one-pivot technique. These teachers usually convey their instructional message to students by telling them to:

1. Keep their heads rock-steady (the head is the swing center).
2. Swing around their spines.
3. Coil and recoil their hips in an imaginary barrel on the backswing and downswing.

If you steady your head and turn around your spine, as I do here, you'll never employ the vital X-Factor backswing moves, and you'll fail to generate power.

I could list some of the instructors who still teach the old single-pivot action, and even tell you the PGA Tour professionals who still believe this is how they swing, when truly it is not. This, however, would serve no purpose, and I have no intention of embarrassing any instructor or pro. Yet, I will say this: My studies and research of the golf swing have been long and extensive. In addition to studying film and videotape of great players of the past, such as Ben Hogan and Sam Snead, I have also traveled extensively to work with the best and the brightest modern-day tour players and teachers from around the world. My conclusion: In good golf swings, there is definitely lateral movement. That observation right there supports the two-pivot theory.

In speaking on behalf of the PGA of America, I have presented my ideas to thousands of club professionals from the United States, the Far East, Europe, and New Zealand. Each time I make it clear that I teach a two-pivot swing. More important, I tell them that they must not teach a system that is basically flawed. Great swingers and top ball strikers do not swing around a fixed point. There is lateral motion in all great swings. It's a fallacy to tell people otherwise. At the Doral Golf Learning Center, where my fellow instructors and I teach the two-pivot swing, I have famous quotations and old sayings posted on the walls. It gives our golf facility a feeling of a football or basketball locker room. There are quotations from legendary sports figures, such as Vince Lombardi, Bill Walsh, and Julius Erving, and ones from the likes of Thoreau and Buddha. One of my favorite sayings is: "Some things have to be believed to be seen." It's just the opposite of the more familiar saying that things have to be seen to be believed. In this book, I'm going to convince you that the two-pivot swing is one of golf's most vital fundamentals. Once you believe it, you will see it in the techniques of all power hitters, perhaps for the first time. You'll also see and understand how other body movements and body angles create the X-Factor, and directly influence the movements of the golf club during the swing; also, how they have a direct effect on the tempo, timing, and rhythm of the swing.

The sooner you understand what we might call the new fundamentals, and groove the X-Factor swing through various drills, the sooner you will hit the ball more powerfully and accurately than ever before. That's a promise!

First—Load the right leg. Get to the back balance point.
Second—Shift
Third—Rotate
Fourth—Throw (Let Go)

THE LAW OF THE ATHLETIC THROW

Once you load your back leg and complete your coil, the forward move is initiated as follows:

First shift weight to the front foot, which basically recenters your body weight. At this stage, the throwing arm is actually still going back, and the right wrist is loading to its fullest.

This is followed by torso rotation and the simultaneous "falling in" of the right arm.

Finally, there is the throw and the extension of the right arm combined with the full weight shift and full rotation of center.

To simplify the athletic throw:
- Shift
- Rotate
- Throw.

BASIC PIVOT ACTIONS
AND THE NATURAL
THROWING MOTION

In order to promote the correct pivoting actions of the body, it's vital that you distribute your weight equally at address—50 percent of your weight on your left foot and leg, 50 percent on your right foot and leg. Also, flex slightly at the knees and bend forward from the hips, in the fashion of a linebacker in the ready position for the snap of the football. You are braced and centered.

On the backswing, your pivot point is your right leg; the idea being to shift the majority of your body weight to your right side. You should feel your weight move to the inside of your right foot and leg—never to the outside—as you coil your hips and shoulders. Principally this is the same windup motion you would use to throw a baseball, football, javelin—or to skip a stone across a pond. In regard to your spine angle, as you complete the windup you should feel as if you turned in a cylinder. The body is wound, ready to spring back.

Pivoting around your right leg, as I do here, is a similar move to one a baseball pitcher uses in the windup.

On the downswing, the idea is to move the lower body (center) laterally, shift weight to your left foot, uncoil your hips and shoulders, and then rotate against the forward pivot point (your left leg). All the time you're shifting and rotating, the arms are responding and preparing for whipping (throwing) the club powerfully into the ball.

On the downswing, the idea is to shift over to your left leg or "pivot point."

FIRST THINGS FIRST

Balance, Balance, Balance!!!

1. Balance at Setup
2. Balance in the Backswing
3. Balance at the Finish

When we take a closer look at body sequencing and body positioning, the chief item on our agenda is balance. More specifically, I would say ready-athletic balance. This dynamic balance must first be established at address. This why I call the "set" position a universal fundamental, and not a step or in-swing checkpoint.

To be in balance and assume an athletic set position, there

The balance "set" position seen from face-on and down-target.

must be pressure on the inside of your arms, legs, and feet.

The proper setup has a distinct feeling of readiness. The body is prepared to move with the club. Athletes have good footwork in any sport they play well. Footwork is a clear fundamental in golf, as it is in all sports, so you must feel your balance through your feet.

The feel in your feet is of weight evenly distributed from the back of the foot to the front of the foot. Most great players I interviewed favored the weight back slightly (more toward the heels). Nobody favored weight toward the toes. Therefore, think of your weight centering on the balls of the feet, or, if anything, just slightly back.

Sense your body weight distributed evenly on each foot. To establish a fifty-fifty set position between the left leg and the right leg, I ask people to imagine they are on two separate weight scales. Further, to feel fifty-fifty, you must elevate your feet slightly, and moderately jockey your feet as you position yourself. You will sense weight flowing between the feet (left and right) only with motion. Watch any good player setting up, and you will immediately see them moving their feet.

Certainly you must avoid freezing the legs at address. Don't allow your weight to favor one side of the body or the other, except for specialty shots.

ANALYZING THE
THROWING MOTION

Many children learn the throwing motion at a very young age. At first, however, they use only the arm. The powerful throw action is learned. Once they add the vital shift and rotate actions, there's a flow to the throw. Then it feels natural. But there's something else they must learn to feel that's even more essential to the throwing action—and to the golf swing. As the right arm is winding up to throw, the lower body must already start moving forward. The same thing must happen in the golf swing. As the player turns the hips and shoulders, and swings the club to the top, the lower body has already started moving in the opposite direction.

Children who play baseball and football, or just learn to throw stones far into a pond, usually turn out to be better golfers than those who never learn the throwing motion. Adults who never played ball sports growing up are often tense golfers with choppy swings. There's often no flow to their swings. It's unnatural. Why? They never learned how to make an athletic throw. As a result, they think out the different segments of the swing. They also hit at the golf ball. Conversely, adults schooled on other sports as youngsters are more relaxed. They can be quickly taught the flow of the swing because they let the ball get in the way of the complete swing. In other words, they swing through it—not at it. They wind up and release the club powerfully and freely just as they released the baseball, football, or stone many years earlier.

It is important to know that once you learn a somewhat effective move, even if it's a physically limiting motion, it becomes natural to you. So if you didn't play sports when you were young, or learn to throw, you are at a distinct disadvantage. You will need to learn the natural "athletic" throwing action required to nail the golf ball.

The body actions involved in skipping a stone across the water's surface are very similar to those in the golf swing. Practicing the "shift" (left), "rotate" (center), and "throw" (right) actions can help you become a more proficient swinger.

THE BODY PRESS

The body press is a subtle movement of the lower body toward the target prior to the takeaway. Therefore, the first move in the swing is actually toward, not away from, the target. Interestingly, most accomplished players are unaware that they make this small shift forward. It is a natural move that becomes a total habit.

Harvey Penick used the image of swinging a bucket or pail of water to illustrate this technical point. To swing the bucket of water, the natural move to create this motion is to start the bucket forward prior to moving it away from the target. To get the pail of water moving smoothly, you need that small motion of the bucket forward.

In golf, teachers are often asked, "What starts the backswing?" I'm going to agree totally with Harvey and most of the top players and instructors I know. To get started smoothly, avoid starting the swing from a dead stop. This tends to greatly increase the chances of a quick or jerky takeaway move and inconsistent rhythm—especially under pressure.

To trigger a good swing:

1. Push off your right instep.
2. Press your right knee forward.
3. Shift your hips gently toward the target.

To help learn this action, you can actually count out numbers in your head. Think of your foot and body action as learning a dance step by the numbers—a-one, and a-two, and a-three. This is a good tip for golfers who get hung up on mechanics. Using the 1-2-3 count will enable you to forget particular positions, and rebound freely into the backswing.

I prefer the body-press action over the commonly recommended hand press, where you push the hands toward the tar-

The commonly recommended "hand press" (left) can cause you to swing the club back on an overly flat plane (right).

get before swinging back. When I see a player press the hands forward, I see a large angle created with the clubshaft. Furthermore, the player tends to exaggerate arm action and lift the club up quickly on a steep plane.

To start back smoothly, move forward first. I say the swing works like this: a micromove forward to start; a minishift to the right in the backswing; then the major shift (move) to the finish.

MOVING CENTER:
ON THE BACKSWING

On the full backswing, your lower center should move a minimum of two to three inches away from the target. That's as we view your belt buckle from face on. Your body's upper center will move much farther—normally about six inches to the right so that it lines up over your right instep. The concept of coiling over your right foot and leg is an ideal swing thought. Use it to help you wind up powerfully.

Over-sliding the hips laterally, in an exaggerated fashion, is definitely a backswing "death move."

In employing your backswing, be careful not to let the lower center move so far to the right that your hips slide or kick out to the right. This fault prevents a good windup, particularly when the head and upper center hang over the top of the ball. Because your coiling action is weak, your shots will not fly very far. Be careful, too, never to let your body's upper and lower centers move forward during the backswing action. This fault prevents you from shifting your weight to the right side. In a reverse pivot you actually shift weight to your left side, then wrongly onto your right foot and leg on the downswing. Because of this pure reverse weight shift, your shots will be drained of power. It's a major power leak.

You don't need to hold a club to practice rotating the right hip in a clockwise direction. Notice how far from "center" my belt buckle moved.

McLEAN'S POWER LEAKS: ON THE BACKSWING

1. Reverse pivot
2. Sliding hips and knees
3. Too much turn in the hips
4. A frozen left arm
5. Arm run-off
6. Collapsing arms
7. Rolling the arms (over-rotating)

The seven top backswing power-leaks:

1. *Reverse pivot*   2. *Hip slide*   3. *Over-rotating hips*

4. Stiff left arm

5. Arm run-off

6. Collapsed left arm with right elbow against body

7. Rolling arms

MOVING CENTER:
ON THE DOWNSWING

On the downswing, your body's lower center (the belt buckle face-on view) should shift toward the target, as much as five to six inches forward of its address position. The average range is three to seven inches. That's a big change from address, and certainly proves that there's lateral motion in the swing. Without question, this is a power move.

I always recall a conversation I had with the great Roberto de Vincenzo about this swing force. I used to watch de Vincenzo and Sam Snead playing senior golf in Orlando in the mid-1970s (when senior golf was almost nothing, just part of the Florida winter tour). Roberto told me that he hit the ball with his stomach. At least, that was the feeling he had when moving his body through the impact zone. What I believe he was feeling was the force of the lower center. I believe he felt the thrust of the club and the center of his body connected together, particularly at impact, when his club was clocked at a speed of around 120 mph. (When the ball is struck, the body's upper center will also have moved forward, although not as much as its lower center. Upper center should be about an inch ahead of address position.)

Roberto's swing concept, involving the stomach, might be a little esoteric. However, because you now know what he really meant, it's a brilliant swing thought to steal from a phenomenal swinger of a club, an extremely long hitter, and one of the greatest players of all time.

In employing the downswing, be careful not to leave your upper center back, or you'll create added tilt in the spine. In turn, your right shoulder will drop dramatically, causing you to swing on an overly shallow in-to-out path. This is a good player's problem, and, believe me, it's a serious one. (See Good Player's Disease, page 95.)

Higher handicappers have the opposite problem: Lower center does not shift. They often let their shoulders initiate the downswing. Consequently, the upper center moves too far forward of the lower body's center. The result of this downswing fault is an overly steep, out-to-in swing path.

The high handicapper's chief fault—body's upper center moves ahead of its lower center—seen from face-on view (left); down-target view (right).

HOW MUCH MOVEMENT: LOWER CENTER

For the top ball strikers, the belt buckle (lower center) will be three to seven inches forward of its address position at impact. The concept that you return the belt buckle to the address location is simply incorrect and will kill your power. There is lateral motion. Measure your lower center movements on videotape, or put a strip of tape on a mirror to monitor this critical action.

NOTE: *According to my studies, John Daly has the biggest lateral move of the belt buckle from address to impact: nine inches. Greg Norman, Fred Couples, and Nick Price are close behind.*

Upper Center

At impact, the upper center will be approximately one inch ahead of its address position (in a full swing). Interestingly, the head has returned to its original location (or maybe even slightly back). You should avoid having the head move in front of its original position. The head will automatically stay in position if the lower body initiates the downswing properly. You won't have to worry about the head moving too far forward if you use your legs correctly in the downswing.

The upper body has not shifted forward nearly as much as the lower body. This then causes a second spine tilt, which is more away from the target than it was at address. Again, don't think about this. Let it happen. I've found conscious thinking on this subject to be particularly detrimental to good golf.

At impact, the body's upper center moves about one inch ahead of its address position; the body's lower center, three to seven inches forward of its original position.

CORRECT HEAD MOVEMENT: ON THE DOWNSWING

In baseball, when facing a fastball pitcher, if the ball gets beyond the body's center, you have no chance of hitting powerfully. If your body and your head are in front of the object you're hitting, you'll only be able to whip at it with your hands and arms. You will not be able to shift and rotate, thus eliminating two major components of power. The same is true in tennis. When the tennis ball is slightly past you, or past the center of your body, you may hit it over the net, but it will be a very weak shot. In fact, often you will mishit it, and not even have the power to carry the net. These illustrations of two sports you may have played (or still play), indicate a fundamental truth. *To hit a ball solidly, you have to be behind it at impact, and be in the process of moving through it.* Remember this the next time you tee up a golf ball.

When your head rotates in front of its starting position, teachers term it "going past the ball" prior to the strike. As a result, it's likely that, to hit the ball squarely and solidly, you will use excessive hand action and not deliver the club quite on the correct attack track. The clubface will usually finish in an open position, causing the ball to fly to the right of target and not very far.

During the Doral Ryder Open in Miami, I conduct very interesting studies to determine whether the pros indeed stay behind the ball at impact. In 1995, there were 144 players in the "field," and all were filmed as they teed off on the twelfth hole, a six-hundred-yard par-five hole. The results of this survey were no less than astonishing. All 144 players stayed behind the ball at impact, with many having their heads farther away from the target than they were at address with the driver. In all my years of teaching, this is one of the few things that I've tested with a 100 percent rating; everyone doing one thing, with no exceptions. Therefore, staying behind the ball (returning your head to its address position, or slightly behind that position) the moment the ball is struck, is truly a fundamental of the power golf swing.

To test your body movement and head position, use this drill: Stand in front of a mirror, crossing your arms in front of (on) your chest. Make a power coil and then unwind center from the ground up, trying to simulate and freeze the ideal body position at impact. Now, check your head position. Ideally, it should be back to its original position or slightly behind its starting position. (To help you make the correct judgment, stick a piece of tape to the mirror in order to mark your starting head position—return to that spot or even slightly behind.)

LOOKING OFF THE BALL

I first became aware of the "looking-off-the-ball" phenomenon as a teenager. It was my own awareness that I need not see the ball at, or even before, impact to hit it very well. Since that time I've read about, and talked with, many professionals and top amateurs who have said they don't see the ball at impact. Very few amateur golfers can even begin to relate, but it's a fact.

In the late 1970s I started to understand why you could look up before impact and hit the ball solidly. I played a tremendous amount of golf in the 1970s with Bob Lendzion, who later won the National Club Pro Championship at PGA West. We talked about the swing incessantly, mostly because I loved Bob's offbeat take on many popularly held views. As Bob improved his game, it became obvious to me that he was look-

Looking off the ball helps certain players make an uninhibited swing and hit tee shots ten to twenty yards farther.

ing down the fairway prior to impact. This was a huge change from his old head-down style of action. Although "Lendz" was a club professional and prolific teacher, he definitely got a lot better with this deliberate move through impact. I was partly responsible for Bob's development of these ideas because I knew the hang-back head-down action looked bad on Lendz and didn't help him. We talked about this often.

Although I had discussed this head-up action with Jimmy Ballard and Ken Venturi, I still needed more evidence before calling this an acceptable new fundamental of the swing. That evidence came my way in 1981, when I played a round of golf at Winged Foot with Hal Sutton and my longtime friend George Zahringer (who dominated golf in the Met area for ten years). Hal and George had become good friends on the amateur circuit.

Sutton was contemplating staying amateur, and becoming sort of a modern day Bobby Jones. As we played, I asked Hal many questions about his game, and was curious to know if he had ever worked with Jimmy Ballard. I asked this question because he had the all-time Ballard look. Hal told me he worked with Floyd Horgen, but yes, he had worked one time with Ballard, at age 17. I then gave Hal some pretty good advice, if I do say so myself. I told him to go see Ballard again and that he should turn pro. After that I watched Hal carefully. The next winter my wife, Justine, and I traveled the tour (I played the winter part of the PGA Tour in 1982), so I saw part of the Sutton growth. Later I watched several lessons Sutton took with Ballard. Of great interest: Hal looked up before impact on many shots. He was the leading money-winner in 1983; the PGA and TPC champion in 1984. I still felt this head-looking-off-the-ball was just an oddity— certainly not something to teach. Yet I saw more good golfers do the same thing, among them, Paul Azinger (another Horgen product).

In 1990, Brad Faxon showed up at Sleepy Hollow. A main feature of Brad's game was the head-down-forever disease, and, as a result, too much hand and wrist action. I began then to teach Brad to look up faster on the downswing, in an effort to get his center and right side to move through the shot. I showed him films that convinced him that the ideas he had been taught as a kid were prohibiting his growth. I never dreamed he would actually be looking down the target line (at the target) before impact in tournaments. Yet eventually, it happened. It's not what I really envisioned, but I did want to stop his faulty hang-back action on the downswing, and his bad habit of staying down too long—a very bad action for a top player. (See Brad's case study on page 98.) It definitely improved his long game.

So, who else looks off the ball? Here's a short list:

ANNIKA SORENSTAM
- 1996 U.S. Open Champion
- 1995 U.S. Open Champion
- 1995 Player of the Year
- 1995 Leading Money Winner

DAVID DUVAL
- 1995 Rookie of the Year
- (Number 10on the PGA Tour money list)

JUSTIN LEONARD
- 1995 Top Tour player (winner of $550,000)
- 1994 U.S. Amateur Champion
- 1993 NCAA Champion

PAUL AZINGER
- Winner of numerous PGA Tour events
- 1993 PGA Champion

STEVE ELKINGTON
- 1995 PGA Champion
- 1995 Vardon Trophy winner

JIM FURYK
- 1996 Hawaiian Open Champion

Every person who first takes up the game is told, "Keep your head down." Is this good advice? I think not. Better to say,

"Watch the ball." Hit it, and watch it go. Don't get stuck looking at a vacant spot on the ground, at the end of what would have to be a very inhibiting swing.

You don't need to see the ball. If you don't believe me, ask the blind golfer, Pat Browne, who breaks eighty regularly.

TO LIFT OR NOT TO LIFT

THE LEFT HEEL MISCONCEPTION

The modern golf swing is being taught, in large part, and by many top instructors, with minimal lower-body action in the backswing.

While I agree with the concept of lower-body resistance, I also believe that far too many people are being taught to minimize footwork. In particular, the notion of keeping the left heel flat on the ground (in the backswing) is now often taught. To some it has become a fundamental.

In reality, keeping the left heel down throughout the golf swing is not a fundamental. I say this because many of the

Here I am making a full body pivot, while keeping my left foot planted. You may find that you'll need to lift your left heel slightly to accomplish the same result.

greatest players and ball strikers lift the left heel. To me, it's hard to dismiss the following list of players who take the left heel (front foot) off the ground on full swings: Ben Hogan, Jack Nicklaus, Byron Nelson, Bobby Jones, Sam Snead, Hale Irwin, Tom Watson, Nick Price, Ben Crenshaw, Johnny Miller, Scott Simpson, Laura Davies. In fact, on the PGA Tour over 30 percent of the players we measured in 1996, at the Doral Ryder Open, lifted their left heel.

To me, this is super-important, because obviously keeping the heel down is an individual matter. Just because Nick Faldo, Fred Couples, Ernie Els, Greg Norman, and others have had success keeping the heel down doesn't make it something every golfer should do. In fact, I believe keeping the heel down on a full driver swing is very negative for the average player. Here's why:

THE ARGUMENT FOR LIFTING THE HEEL

1. Most people are not supple enough to make a full 90-degree shoulder turn while keeping the left heel down.
2. We feel much of our rhythm through our feet. Lifting and replanting the left heel promotes the correct sequence and good footwork.
3. Good footwork is the mark of all champions in all sports.
4. Most golfers make a much better weight shift when they tend to lift the heel slightly.
5. Golfers who leave the heel down tend to swing flat-footed and overuse the upper body.

WHAT TO GUARD AGAINST

Lifting the heel too much is almost always negative. How high is the limit? Jack Nicklaus lifted the heel higher than any great player—often six inches or so, on drives. Yet Nicklaus is generally regarded as the longest, straightest driver in the history of the game, and many would contend the greatest driver of all time.

When the left heel is raised, the left knee responds. Usually raising the heel too high causes overuse of the legs in the backswing. The result is a loss of lower-body resistance. The golfer turns his hips too far around, slides his hips, or the left knee pops directly out toward the target line. All three of these moves are serious mistakes.

So, too high is usually anything over two to three inches. That seems to be the maximum for most golfers—but there are exceptions. John Daly, for example, lifts his heel like Nicklaus, yet has great lower-body action. Other supple players, like those previously mentioned, create a full upper-body pivot while keeping the heel planted. This is great if you can do it.

The full-figure view (left) and the close-up view (right) show how lifting the heel too much can cause overuse of the legs ("loose legs") and overuse of the hips (twisting).

What You Should Feel and Do

On your full power swings (long irons and woods), weight should roll off the instep of your left (front) foot. Weight should transfer diagonally into the right foot and right leg. Weight transfers into a braced right leg. As the upper body coils, it pulls the lower body around as well. Thus, the left heel is pulled off the ground because of a full coil. It is not lifted independently.

At the top of a full-body pivot, 70 to 85 percent of your weight has shifted to the back leg, behind the golf ball, and the shoulders have turned 90 degrees or more. Your weight shift is best felt through good footwork. Raising the heel greatly helps this goal for many golfers.

When the change of direction occurs, one of golf's greatest keys to initiate the correct sequence can be the left heel that

If your heels shift away from the target on the downswing, cure your "death move" action by lifting the left heel, on the backswing, then replanting it where it started. Spend a lot of time on correct footwork techniques.

triggers this move. Sequence! Sequence! Sequence! The main goal of this book is to show you how to use your body correctly. Feeling your golf swing through good footwork, and possibly lifting the left heel, is a link to improving your rhythm and timing.

In the all-important move to start the downswing, it is the lower body that must lead the parade. Replanting the left heel is a tremendous key to feeling and understanding this critical move.

In my research, many of golf's greatest players have used this one swing thought as a fundamental to starting the downswing. Replanting the left heel only works when the heel is taken off the ground in the first place. You can't replant a heel that was never lifted.

This trigger to initiate the downswing was almost a universally accepted axiom. However in recent years it has lost favor. I believe this is due to a few golfers who have been successful keeping it down, but it does not apply to the great majority.

DEATH MOVE

Occurs when the left hip has moved away from the target prematurely in the downswing, with the result being a come-over action—the upper body moves ahead of the lower. *Cure:* Be sure to lift the left heel slightly, then replant it where it started as a sequence key.

SEEING IS BELIEVING

In 1980, while analyzing swings of pro golfers on video, Carl Welty showed me how to draw on the television screen. No teachers were doing this at the time, so I kept it a secret for as long as I could. It was such a tremendous advantage. Now I use the computer and a special software package I helped develop. It is quite advanced, yet the old, dry-erase pen worked just as well.

Using the pen on the TV screen allowed me to see things much more clearly. It became possible to measure and track where the clubhead traveled throughout the backswing and downswing. Carl called it an X ray. Like a doctor studying the implications of each X ray, Carl and I would diagnose the arcs and positions of every top player in the world. I loved that term and loved the fact nobody else in the world knew about it.

Carl and I found that the arc or plane of the backswing varied tremendously. There was no distinct pattern and no common fundamentals. Then, I began to look solely at the shaft. All of a sudden, I saw a common denominator. Almost every top player's shaft reacted the same way. On the backswing the shaft tended to work more vertically than on the downswing.

During the second half of the swing, the shaft would fall, or lie down slightly. Most importantly, I didn't ever see the opposite. That means no top player had a shaft that worked from flat to steep. Surprisingly, the correct action is a very natural action and corresponds closely to the action of a baseball hitter. Tour pros who have a tremendous shaft drop or fall include Calvin Peete (ten times the PGA Tour leader in Driving Accuracy and Greens In Regulation), Lee Trevino, Nick Price, and many other accurate players.

I termed this phenomenon "The X" and spoke about it during workshops that I conducted around the country for the PGA. The clubshaft, when drawn from the target line, went up somewhat vertically, then flattened on the downswing, forming an X on paper. (The X-Factor, as you will learn, is something quite different.)

POWER COMPONENTS

I like to look at the golfer as a machine, having four key components.

The first component is the golf club, the device we strike the ball with. For the advanced player, the club is swung with abandon. We hit with the club, but it is powered by the body.

The second key component is the wrists. They hinge and set on the backswing, and release on the downswing. Soft wrists, at address, are fundamental to creating high clubhead speed and power in the golf swing.

The third key component is the arms, which attach to the body, the fourth component and engine of the golfer-machine. The arms must work with the body in unison. It is very easy for the arms to disconnect from the body action. However, through proper practice, any golfer can begin to coordinate the big muscles of the body to the independent swing of the arms, wrists, and club. The arms must not work independently.

The fourth key component is the body. The body should move in a small space, and its movements should be simple. It is often useful to think of your body movements as a dance step. The logic behind this is that you feel rhythm, weight shift, and pressure through your feet. Then connect the arms, wrists, and club to this powerful and efficient engine.

SEE PAGES 40–41.
When you compare the "no-club" swing (first four photos) to the "club swing" (last four photos), you can appreciate how the club is powered by the body.

ASSEMBLING THE ENGINE

The basic body I'll describe has three main sections. First is the lower body. From the bottom of your spine, the body splits off with your two legs each connecting to the earth. The legs are bent slightly at the knees and braced solidly against the ground. Good footwork and proper leg action are two key swing fundamentals. As I've mentioned, you will feel weight shift mainly through your feet and legs. When you know what to do, the shift of the weight is not dramatic and it is precisely equivalent to the natural throwing motion used by many children.

The next part of the engine is the upper body (the thorax). This includes your shoulders, pecs, lats, spine, and the abdominal area. It also includes the two body centers, your lower body center (just below the belly button), and your upper body center (your sternum). In my teaching I watch how much these centers move, when they move, and how fast they move.

On the backswing, the upper spine moves to the right, while the lower tip of the spine barely moves at all.

Viewing from the face-on angle, on the downswing, the lower center moves considerably forward—approximately three to six inches forward of its address position. I usually monitor the belt buckle as I examine how far center shifts. The upper center, which moves much farther to the right in the backswing, will not be nearly as far forward at impact. The golfer's upper center will be only about one inch forward of its address position. It is not behind its address position as many teachers believe. These observations prove that there is lateral motion in a good swing, and that the lower body initiates it on the forward swing.

The body's upper center is controlled by the shoulders; the lower center by the hips. I've used these two centers to determine motion. Without a doubt, correct use of the body allows us to hit hard, stay in balance, and give the appearance of minimal effort.

The third part of the body's engine is the very upper part of the spine and the head. In the model setup, the spine is not straight, as many people perceive it to be. At a point between the top of the shoulder blades, the spine begins to curve forward. There is actually a bend of between 10 and 30 degrees from the upper spine to the top of the head. This is tremendously important because it has much to do with relaxed shoulders and an absence of tension in the neck. This is critical to developing speed and the correct axis tilt of the shoulders.

The head rotates and/or shifts away from the target on the backswing, allowing your shoulders more freedom to turn. Also, the upper body coils over a braced lower body. On the forward swing the head may drop slightly or move back of its address position due to the thrust of both the hip and weight-shifting actions. The head is merely responding, counterbalancing the lateral movements of your body's center.

If the body is to work as a powerful engine, on the backswing, its upper part must coil over a braced lower part.

THE POWER COIL:
BREAKING IT DOWN

KNEES

Most amateurs pay little attention to the knees, despite the fact that they are vital to a proper coil. Don't believe it? Try turning your lower body without moving your knees. It can't be done.

At the top of the swing, the line across your knees should point about 25 degrees to the right of the target. Don't let the right knee straighten or you'll overturn. If your knees aren't turning enough, stop letting your left foot stay glued to the

This photograph will give you a clear picture of how the knees, hips, shoulders, and head are positioned at address.

These two photographs will allow you to form a clear picture of how the knees, hips, shoulders, and head move during the backswing's power-coil action.

ground. Allowing the left heel to lift during the backswing will activate your knees.

Hips

A good turn of the knees allows the hips to turn and promotes transfer of weight to the right side. The hips should turn to between 40 and 65 degrees by the time you reach the top of the swing, out-turning the knees by approximately a two-to-one margin. To trigger a good hip turn, Greg Norman thinks of turning his right hip pocket behind him in a clockwise direction, almost directly back—no twist, no slide.

Shoulders

When you think of a turn or coil, most golfers think of shoulders, yet it is the proper coiling of the hips that contributes to a big shoulder turn. If the hips rotate 60 degrees, the shoulders can still reach 100 degrees or more rotation in a full swing, which will produce tremendous torque. Few golfers can attain this large differential, but those are good goals and will translate into power and distance.

Head

Yes, the head really turns, moves, or even turns and moves, even though you've probably heard for years that it must remain stock still. Not true. A good way to think about it is that the chin has its own little swing. In a model backswing the chin should rotate about 20 to 25 degrees. If it doesn't, the shoulders won't have the freedom to turn fully.

I know there are many people out there who think of the head as a stationary post, and are trying to swing around a fixed center. This is a controversial point, yet it is a point that I want to make very clear. The greatest players in the world turn or move their heads, and most move them to the right (on the backswing), when swinging any club from a mid-iron to the driver. That's a fact.

Now, if the bottom of the player's head doesn't turn at all, it will at least move over to the right, away from the target. For

Compare the head position at address (left) to the head position at the top of the backswing (right), and you'll see how much it rotates.

a very right-eyed dominant person, that's a possibility (Ben Crenshaw, Paul Azinger). The reason being: Turning the head and nose can cause the right-eyed dominant, right-handed golfer to actually lose sight of the ball.

For golfers who tend to reverse pivot to promote the proper head movement, imagine an outline of a second head, one-half your size, to the right of your own. On the backswing, simply turn into that "second" head.

ANGLES AT ADDRESS

Upright spine angle

The angle you see between the arms and the clubshaft indicates that the wrists are cocked at address.

Standard spine angle

The arms do not hang straight down, as many teachers advocate. In fact, when setting up to play all long clubs, the arms hang on an angle, out and away from the body.

When standing behind a player who is squarely aligned, you should only see one leg and one arm.

Note that the player's spine is not straight to the top of the head. Note, too, that the player's head is tilted down slightly.

IGNITION

The swing's first move: The body press.

Prior to taking the club away, make a "micro-shift" toward the target.

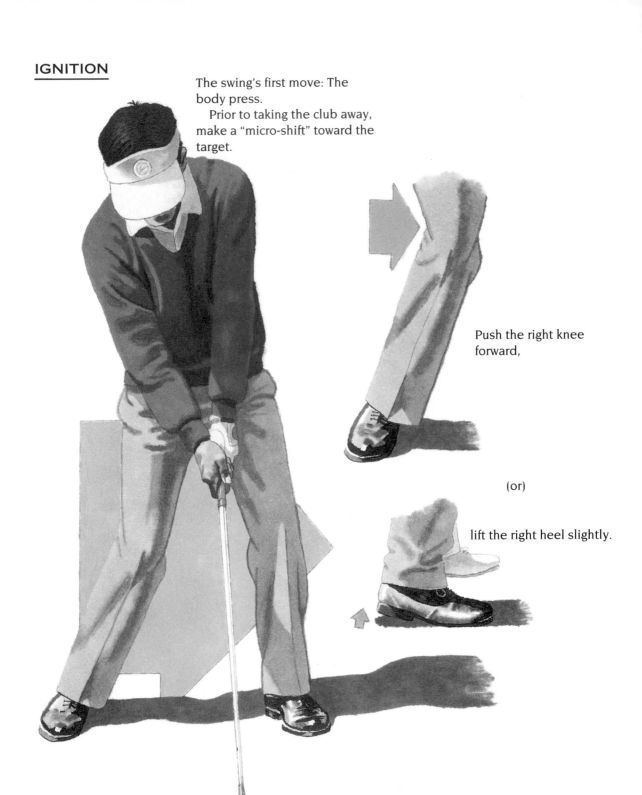

Push the right knee forward,

(or)

lift the right heel slightly.

THE PERFECT TAKE-AWAY

Weight rolls from front foot to back foot. The left knee rotates inward, only slightly.

The imaginary triangle, formed by the shoulders, arms, and hands, allows the player to take the club away in one piece while maintaining the flex in the right knee.

Notice how the hands stay below the belt-line, the right elbow is free from the body (but beginning to bend), and the shoulders have out-turned the hips.

As you take the club away you may sense a move to the side rather than around (see above). As you swing back, you should feel the right elbow "float."

COMPLETING THE BREAKAWAY

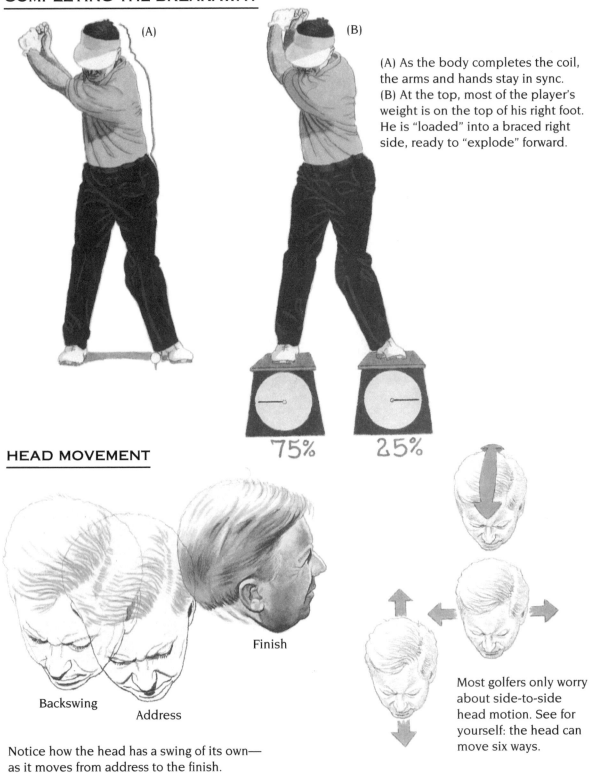

(A)

(B)

(A) As the body completes the coil, the arms and hands stay in sync.
(B) At the top, most of the player's weight is on the top of his right foot. He is "loaded" into a braced right side, ready to "explode" forward.

75%   25%

HEAD MOVEMENT

Finish

Backswing

Address

Notice how the head has a swing of its own— as it moves from address to the finish.

Most golfers only worry about side-to-side head motion. See for yourself: the head can move six ways.

RIGHT HIP BACK

Death Move #1: The right hip kicks out.

Death Move #2: The hips overturn, causing the majority of the player's weight to stay left. The classic reverse pivot.

Take a page out of Greg Norman's lesson book to help you make a solid hip coil. Norman thinks R.H.B. before he swings. So should you. See how this thought allows the player (above) to turn his Right Hip Back behind himself.

THE X-FACTOR

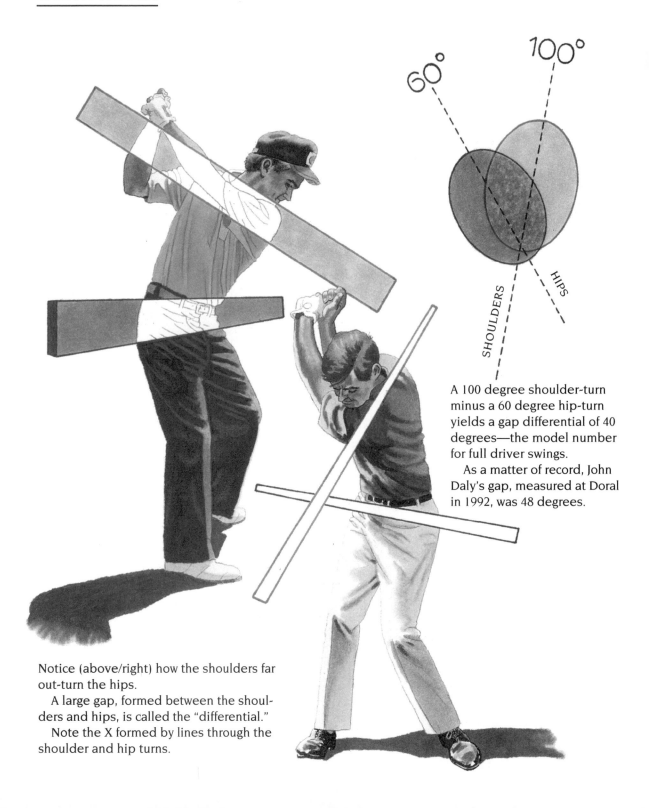

60° 100°

SHOULDERS

HIPS

A 100 degree shoulder-turn minus a 60 degree hip-turn yields a gap differential of 40 degrees—the model number for full driver swings.

As a matter of record, John Daly's gap, measured at Doral in 1992, was 48 degrees.

Notice (above/right) how the shoulders far out-turn the hips.

A large gap, formed between the shoulders and hips, is called the "differential."

Note the X formed by lines through the shoulder and hip turns.

LEFT-ARM ANGLES

Notice the different left-arm angles at the top of the swing: IDEAL, too flat, too upright.

Too flat   IDEAL   Too upright

The shaft angle at address (far left), and your left-arm angle at the top (near left) should parallel each other.

AT-THE-TOP POSITIONS

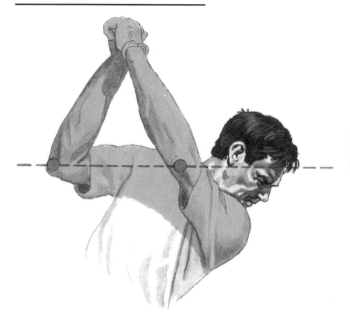

(Left) In a power swing the elbows should be level or nearly level. A triangle should be formed once the player reaches the top.

The at-the-top triangle

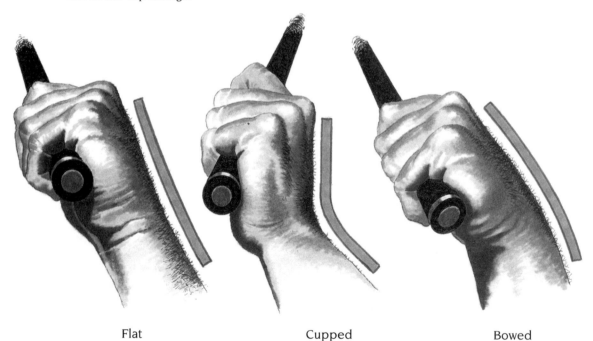

Flat　　　　　　Cupped　　　　　　Bowed

Ideally, at the top of a model golf swing, the left wrist would be nearly "flat." However, this is not the secret to great ball-striking.

Your grip, at address, and hand configuration, have a lot to do with whether you arrive in a flat, cupped, or bowed position.

INCREASING THE X-FACTOR

As the shoulders and arms are still going back, the lower body reverses direction.

At this point in the swing, many players feel weight being pushed downward into their right leg. Others feel the left knee, right knee, or both knees start forward.

To appreciate this unique technical point, notice how the body's lower center (dot) is moving forward.

As the shoulders turn, and the lower body reverses direction, the X-factor differential, or gap, is increased.

Coil your "upper" over a braced "lower" to simplify your backswing.

The lower half reverses direction. The upper half responds. The correct move is for the right shoulder to lower the hands. The hands go down before they go forward.

THE THROW (AND DIFFERENT L-POSITIONS)

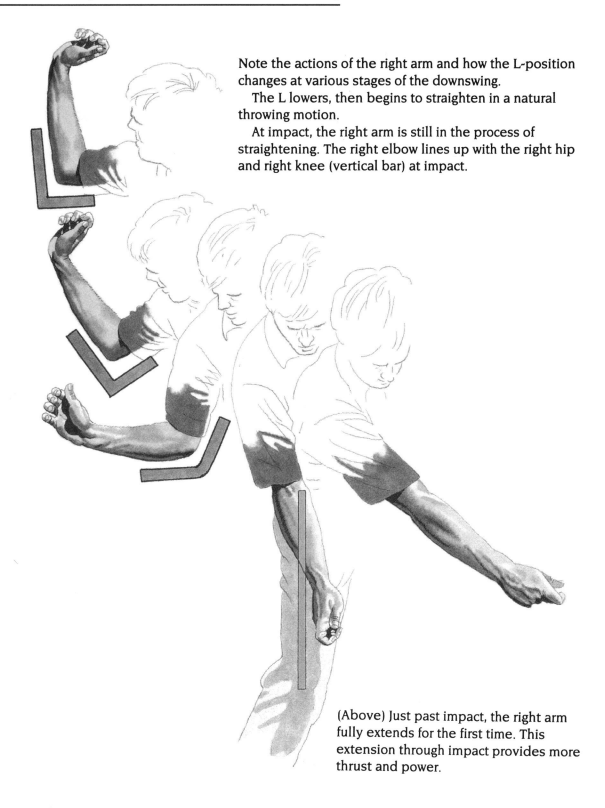

Note the actions of the right arm and how the L-position changes at various stages of the downswing.

The L lowers, then begins to straighten in a natural throwing motion.

At impact, the right arm is still in the process of straightening. The right elbow lines up with the right hip and right knee (vertical bar) at impact.

(Above) Just past impact, the right arm fully extends for the first time. This extension through impact provides more thrust and power.

POWER POINTERS FROM "THE MICK"

Technically, the shifting action the late Mickey Mantle uses here, to step into a pitched ball, is similar to a golfer's downswing.

75ol° 25ol°   50ol°   50ol°

Loaded

Two-way change of direction. Upper going back, lower going forward.

25ol°   75ol°

The hit   Extension

THE SIT-DOWN

Here's what happens when the player arrives in the sit-down position:

- The left knee shuttles forward, toward the target.
- The right knee kicks out, toward the ball.
- Both knees appear to "separate," the player's body weight is recentered.
- The shoulders respond to the actions of the lower body—following, not leading.

Freeze this downswing position. Then, place a club across your thighs. If you've employed the proper sit-down action, it should point at the target.

LOADING/UNLOADING YOUR POWER

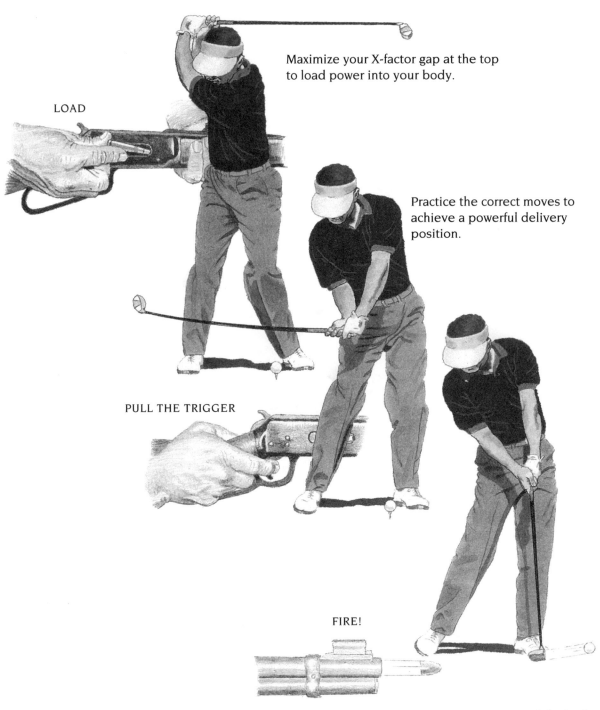

LOAD

Maximize your X-factor gap at the top to load power into your body.

Practice the correct moves to achieve a powerful delivery position.

PULL THE TRIGGER

FIRE!

Proper sequencing of the body allows you to explode through impact.

PERSONALIZE YOUR FOOT POSITIONS

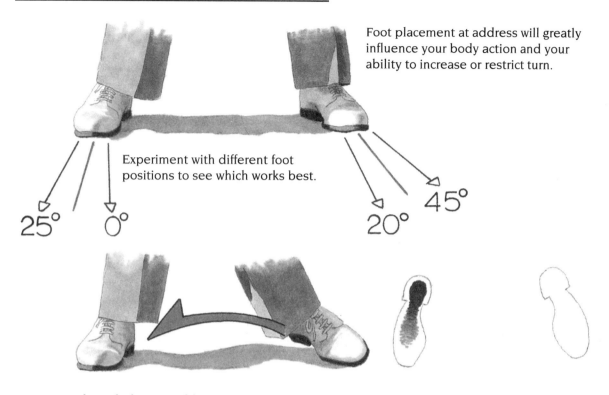

Foot placement at address will greatly influence your body action and your ability to increase or restrict turn.

Experiment with different foot positions to see which works best.

25°   0°   20°   45°

Above/below: Good foot positions trigger solid weight shifting actions: off the inside of your left foot on the backswing, off the inside of your right foot on the downswing.

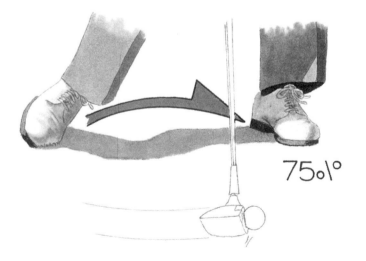

75o\°

In a full swing the right heel should be off the ground at impact.

A TRUE GOLF FUNDAMENTAL

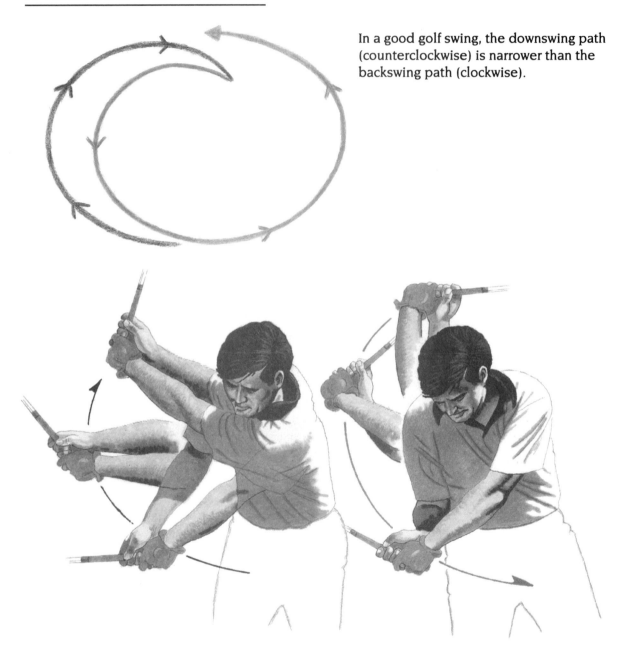

In a good golf swing, the downswing path (counterclockwise) is narrower than the backswing path (clockwise).

To increase clubhead speed and hit the ball powerfully, think "wide back" and "narrow down."

The combination of a lateral shift and passive hands will **help you** narrow the downswing path.

RETURNING TO IMPACT

KNEES

Every turn that goes one way in the backswing must recoil coming down. You will notice that while the turns begin in the same position at address, at impact they are dissimilar. Don't make the mistake of thinking address and impact are mirror images. If you do, you won't close the gaps on the four turns, and as a result you won't be hitting with power.

Before the knees rotate on the downswing, they must make enough lateral shift to transfer weight from the right to the left side. As a result, the knees can be as much as 30 to 40 degrees open at impact.

HIPS

The hips out-turn the knees on the backswing. However, by impact they are almost in line, pointing left of the target, usually between 10 and 30 degrees open.

There must be lateral movement of the hips to transfer the weight from the right side to the left side, but the majority of the hip movement is rotational. The position of the hips at impact is more forward and more open than it was at address.

SHOULDERS

A close-up view of knee and hip action at impact.

By impact the shoulders have almost caught up to the hips and knees, pointing slightly left of the target. That's quite a gap to close from the top of the swing, and it's all turn. The shoulders do not slide. They catch up because they are pivoting around a single axis, the spine, while the hips turn over two pivot points, the feet. The hips thus have both lateral and rotational movement.

To eliminate upper body slide, work on retaining your spine angle through impact. Stay in the cylinder. This will enable you to release the club with your body; as a result, your hands go left after impact, rather than swinging out toward the target. That's the mark of a true turning swing. The hands, arms, and club stay in front of center. When you get it, you will experience a fantastic feeling of connection and power.

HEAD

The one turn that is allowed to match its address position is that of the head. That means you're staying behind the ball. But if your head shifts past its original position, your upper body and head have moved ahead of the ball at impact, and that spells trouble.

SMASHING THE GOLF BALL: HEAD POSITION

A critical aspect of smashing the golf ball (or "squashing" the golf ball as Tom Kite would say) is that your upper center is slightly forward. Your head, however, returns to position. So the head actually has the effect of being more off the right side of the body. You must almost consciously look up to the target quickly after impact or risk the chance of hanging back too long. Allow the body to take the head where it should go. Do not restrict the head by forcing it to stay down after impact, which will lead to loss of both power and control.

When you practice in front of a mirror, closely monitor your head position relative to your back, shoulders, and/or upper center.

Remember, of all the body angles and body positions, only a few things at impact resemble address. The head is one of them. Anyone thinking you return to your address position at impact is operating in total darkness.

Through impact, the head essentially is more off to the right side of the body.

Let the head release. Do not restrict the head by forcing it to stay down, after impact.

WHAT YOU MUST KNOW

If I had the chance to work with you in a private lesson or at one of my golf schools, I would get you to experience the athletic set I've described in this book.

Next, I would hammer in the belief that golf corresponds closely to other physical activities you do. That would include throwing a rock into a lake, chopping down a tree, hitting a baseball, or hundreds of other activities.

The body movements required for good golf are very similar to other things you have already done. Golf is not different, as many books and teachers would have you believe. Therefore, I would have you demonstrate other physical activities to improve your understanding of the golf swing. One thing we could do is throw a club down the range or simply use a right-arm-only tossing drill.

LEARN THE BASIC BODY MOVES

First would be to load the right side in your backswing; create a gap between your shoulder turn and your hip turn. Then start your forward swing in the same way any athlete would go forward in any other sport. That is, Shift, Rotate, Throw.

The forward-swing start is the make-or-break move for having any chance of delivering a consistently powerful blow.

From the top of the properly loaded backswing, start the lower half of your body first. This lateral shift action will cause the right shoulder to lower, as it must. As the right shoulder lowers, the right elbow will track down-plane on the correct initial attack track.

This move is virtually identical to the action all Little Leaguers will have as they field a ground ball and make the side-arm throw over to first base. Ben Hogan wrote about the action of the right arm and right hand in his great book, *Five*

As Ben Hogan pointed out, the right elbow plays a very critical role in the downswing.

Lessons. Hogan described and illustrated this throwing action in detail. He wrote,

> In its general character, the correct motion of the right arm and hand in the impact area resembles the motion an infielder makes when he throws half side-arm, half underhand to first after fielding a ground ball. As the right arm swings forward, the right elbow is very close to the right hip and leads the arm—it is the part of the arm nearest the target.

MORE ON HOGAN AND LITTLE LEAGUE

As Hogan led into this athletic throw metaphor, he wrote that as he started down, he only thought of two things: "starting the hips back and then hitting just as hard as I can with the upper part of my body, my arms and hands, in that order."

The good news to remember is this: Learn or relearn the basic throwing action. No Little Leaguers think about lowering their right side or leading their throw with the elbow. If they did, they wouldn't do very well. The kids just shuffle forward, turn their bodies, and make the throw with no conscious effort. That's the action you will want to practice: the athletic throw. It's the same move in golf.

Use your body properly, and the result is you can swing your arms and hands freely. Your arms and the club will seek the correct plane much easier.

A NOTE ON LITTLE LEAGUERS

When children begin throwing, they usually require some training or instruction. With a little help from mom or dad, the child will soon develop a nice throwing action. Remember, it's not automatic. Even throwing a baseball over to first base takes practice.

MORE ON HOGAN

Ben Hogan is put into a category of ball striking that few, if any, other golfers have achieved. I also believe that Hogan was way ahead of his time in golf knowledge. His descriptions and writings about golf, over 40 years ago, are still astonishing to read.

Hogan wrote this: "The hips initiate the downswing." Followed by:

> To begin the downswing, turn your hips back to the left. There must be enough lateral motion forward to transfer the weight to the left foot. The path the hips take on the backswing is not the exact same path they traveled as they were turned on the backswing. On the downswing, their "arc" should be a trifle wider—both in regard to the amount of lateral motion and the amount of eventual rotation around the rear.

Most people apparently miss this important paragraph when we talk about Hogan's concepts. Most people I've talked to think Hogan said, "turn the hips back to the left," or a pure rotary motion.

In studying Hogan's swing in person and thousands of times on tape, I can tell you Hogan didn't do that. He had tremendous lateral thrust. Plus you can read for yourself in a direct quote from his book that Hogan talked about weight shift and lateral motion. "You could look it up," to quote Yogi Berra.

Hogan also has a wonderful little line in *Five Lessons*: "The body swings the arms." You'll have to think about that one for a little while. Then move on with this Hogan line: "The action of the arms is motivated by the movements of the body."

Among other ideas, these words provide extremely valuable clues to the secrets of golf.

THROWING PRINCIPLES

$\mathbf{T}$he fact that a player can employ an unorthodox backswing position, yet hit the ball squarely and solidly, should teach you one important thing: It's the move from the top of the backswing that separates the good ball striker from the poor ball striker.

Examine the backswing positions of Ben Hogan, Sam Snead, Arnold Palmer, Jack Nicklaus, Nancy Lopez, Bruce Lietzke, Phil Mickelson, Johnny Miller, Tom Watson, Nick Faldo, Corey Pavin, and Lee Trevino. At the top of the swing, they look different—especially the length of the swing, shaft location, and clubface position.

The similarity, my friends, is in the change of direction from the top of the backswing to the move down to impact. This is when Miller and Faldo turn their open clubface to square, while Palmer, Trevino, and Watson turn their closed clubface to square at the start down.

From the top of the backswing, the clubhead and clubshaft react automatically to certain movements of the body. There is no conscious directing or manipulating of the club by the top players. The move from the top of the backswing is a chain reaction. It must occur in a sequence. The problem is that the sequence can be sensed in different ways by individual players. This is what confuses the amateur. For example, all a top pro has to say or write about, in a book or a magazine article, is that he feels as if he whips the club into the ball with his hands, and a nation of golfers is put on the wrong track.

It is your hands that hold the club. It is your arms that guide the path. Yet, it is the improper use of the hands and arms that causes most golfers to swing on an outside-in path, instead of attacking the ball on an inside track.

After teaching golf for over 20 years, and using high-speed cameras and videotape constantly, the biggest difference I see between the hacker and the accomplished player is the way they start the forward move in golf. The pro is patient and depends on the proper sequencing of the body to take him into and through the impact zone. The typical amateur, by contrast, impatiently hits from the top, either with the hands and arms or by spinning the shoulders. By starting incorrectly, the amateur has no chance to deliver the clubhead into the ball with power and consistency.

The first move from the top must be with the lower body. Furthermore, to swing into impact, with power, you must adhere faithfully to those principles involved in every other physical throwing or hitting motion: shift, rotate the body center, release the right arm. You cannot defy the law of the athletic throw if you are to hit a golf ball long and straight. You must make a lateral shift or "bump," with the left side, then fire the right side. When you employ these actions, you don't have to think about pulling the club downward. You may feel pull in the left arm due to body rotation, but you must not consciously pull the left arm. Correct body actions ensure that the arms will whip the club powerfully into impact (from the inside) with the sweet spot of the clubface squarely meeting the back center portion of the ball.

EFFORTLESS POWER VERSUS POWERLESS EFFORT

When the body movements are employed correctly, the swing motion is surprisingly simple. Now I did not say it is simple to learn. Like many things in life, simplicity is not easy to come by.

All the great athletes tend to make their sport look easy. But this is particularly true in golf. When you watch Fred Couples and most other professionals, it is almost depressing. They smash the golf ball with incredible power, yet appear to expend minimal effort.

What's fascinating about watching pros swing a club is the differences in their backswing actions. At the top, some tour pros set the clubshaft parallel to the target line, while others cross the line (clubshaft points well right of target) or lay the club off (clubshaft points well left of target). The parallel position of the club, at the top of the backswing, is therefore not a true fundamental of the swing. As Jackie Burke always told me: "If all we had to do to be a great ball striker is point the club down the target line, with a square clubface at the top of the backswing, everybody would be great." Pointing the clubshaft down the target line at the top of the backswing is simply not that tough to do. The reality is that this does not ensure that you are going to be a good ball striker, or a long ball striker, or a straight ball hitter. It is not the secret to greatness.

Some pros swing relatively fast. Some pros swing relatively slowly. All the swings on the tour, however, have rhythm. That's not the only similarity. All pros use the same basic body sequencing. Granted, they feel different things when they swing; but make no mistake, they all abide by the laws of natural human athletic motion. Whether you watch John Daly or Jack Nicklaus, Fred Couples or Fred Funk, Tom Kite or Tom Lehman, Justin Leonard or Annika Sorenstam, they all depend on a shift-and-rotate action, combined with a free arm swing, which allows them all to arrive in similar impact positions with power.

I remember my good friend and great teacher/player, Bob Toski, always used the phrase "effortless power vs. powerless effort" in describing the difference between the expert golfer and the weekend hacker.

What Toski observed is a fact. The amateur actually overuses the body. Often the higher handicapper turns more on the back-swing, and uses more leg action than the accomplished player. On the downswing, he or she starts with the wrong sequence, often using the shoulders and arms to guide the clubface to the golf ball. The result is usually a weak mishit.

The typical professional uses far less effort and energy on the backswing, yet winds up powerfully. On the forward swing, he or she moves the lower center first, and uses efficient leg action to help generate high clubhead speed, which explains why the pros' shots fly more powerfully and accurately.

To learn and groove the fundamental body actions of the swing, perform the actions slowly, one at a time. I keep backing students up until they can employ—and feel—a correct and successful action of the swing. It is a building-block approach that helps students learn faster, and it's an approach that they soon appreciate. When they see themselves swinging on video, they usually feel very good about the accomplishment.

VITAL UPPER LEFT ARM MOVEMENTS

The upper left arm slides slightly across and up the chest on the backswing.

At impact, and through the early follow-through, the upper left arm must be glued to the chest. The upper left arm does not rotate.

Practice keeping the left arm glued to your chest, without holding a club, to get a feel for the proper "connected" action.

THE VITAL LEFT WRIST POSITION

A GOLF FUNDAMENTAL

The left wrist must not break down. It must stay as firm as "Bethlehem Steel," as Claude Harmon, Sr., the 1948 Masters' champion, used to say. This is how you achieve power in the swing.

The rotation of the body center is the most important key to maintaining a flat or bowed left wrist. The second most important key is developing a shallow angle of attack (as opposed to a steep angle of attack).

The vital left wrist position at impact. As 1948 Masters champion Claude Harmon Sr. pointed out, "It should be like Bethlehem steel."

QUICK TIPS FOR GENERATING HIGH CLUBHEAD SPEED

Some other power secrets shared by the PGA Tour's long drivers are:

1. Relax the wrists.
2. Hold the club with moderate to light grip pressure, 5 on my 1–10 grip-o-meter (1 super light—10 super tight).
3. Soften the arms;
4. Use a two-pivot point swing, using center to shift and rotate.
5. Visualize the three key X-Factor positions: top of the backswing (the power coil), impact, and finish.

In generating clubhead speed, visualize the three vital X-Factor positions—at the top (left), at impact (center), in the finish (right)—before you swing.

THE HIPS RISE

As you come into the impact zone, with all systems go, your hips will actually rise. That's correct: The hips (or your hip line) are higher at impact than at address. They will continue to rise higher as you go to the full finish position.

You might ask, "If my hips rise, do my head and shoulders rise too?" The answer: No. You can stay in your spine angle and keep your head level while straightening your left leg and/or raising your hips at impact.

To hit hard you'll need to learn this important power key. To hit down and through you need to be up. This seemingly

Coming into impact (left), and through impact (right), the hips should rise.

illogical concept is actually a fundamental truth. Conversely, if your hip line drops and your right side drops with it, you will always be hitting up on the ball, and never deliver a maximum power blow.

To sum it up, the upper part of your body stays level as the lower half rises, coming into impact and providing added leverage. Both the upper and lower body will stand up. To deliver a downward blow with your irons, you need to move forward and stay up—just the opposite of what the amateur golfer will logically think and probably do.

In working extensively with Tom Kite since 1992, we talked in detail about his left leg and left knee action. Tom always tended to slide the knee too far and dip the knees excessively. He has worked hard to hit into a braced left leg and a straighter left leg. As a result, he picked up a lot of speed and distance.

It is very important to remember you can overdo this. If the left hip does not bump forward, and spins instead, the left leg will lean too far away from the target and this will cause you to pull across the ball.

PART II

THE X-FACTOR

THE X-FACTOR: A PREVIEW

Whenever I teach amateur players, chat with them at the nineteenth hole about their games or a hot new ball, talk with them at tournaments, or fit them for a new titanium-headed driver, I'm reminded of the golfer's obsession with power. I'm also made aware of their misconceptions on how to produce longer tee shots.

Nine out of ten players think that they should turn their shoulders and hips more, and the harder they whale at the ball, the farther it will fly. It is possible they still haven't heard about the X-Factor discovery we made in 1992 with Mike McTeigue, and his SportSense Motion Trainer (SMT).

Back then, we strapped the SMT to the player's back, then had him or her swing. The unit on the player's back sent information to a computer, which yielded data on the hip and shoulder turns. Furthermore, video was taken of the pro swinging. When a particular player appeared on the television screen swinging to the top, one line was drawn across the hips,

The X-Factor discovery couldn't have been made without the SportSense Motion Trainer (SMT) shown here. I'm the guinea pig. Mike McTeigue is at the controls.

another across the shoulders. The converging lines formed an X, and showed the various gap angles.

After testing many top tour pros on the SMT machine, I helped disprove this widely accepted fundamental of the swing: "To generate maximum power, turn your hips and shoulders to the max."

Our discovery: The generation of high clubhead speed and power in the golf swing has a direct relationship to the creation of a gap, or differential, between the shoulder and hip turn. In general, the bigger the differential, the farther you hit the ball.

What was even more interesting about the SMT data was that not one power hitter turned his shoulders precisely 90 degrees and his hips 45 degrees (previously thought to be the ideal power-generating combination). For example, John Daly turned his shoulders 114 degrees, his hips 66 degrees; the gap being 48 degrees (114 minus 66 equals 48). Of all the pros tested, Daly had the highest "gap number." Daly is, of course, the PGA Tour's longest hitter. Lennie Clements and Mike Reid, two of the shortest hitters on tour, had gap numbers of 27 and 30 respectively (two of the lowest). Since then I've worked several times with Lennie on improving his body pivot. When Lennie saw those numbers in <u>GOLF</u> Magazine, he told me the light went on for him. I know he feels the improvements he's made with his pivot have helped him to hit the ball longer.

In measuring the tour pros' hip and shoulder rotation on the SMT, we found that all long hitters do not necessarily make big shoulder turns. Nor do all players who make big turns hit the ball a long way. However, every long hitter tested had a big differential—rotating his shoulders much more than his hips. More important, the big hitter's differential comes from a higher percentage of his upper body turn. What does this all mean? *Simple—it's how you turn, not how much you turn.*

As for swinging faster and hitting harder, this often creates more disasters than distance. Timing, tempo, and technique are all sacrificed when you step on the gas too fast. Your swing may be a blur and you may create incredible force at impact, but the chances are the force is misdirected and the clubhead isn't square, leading to terrible results. Remember these words of John Jacobs, the great British teacher: "Power is clubhead

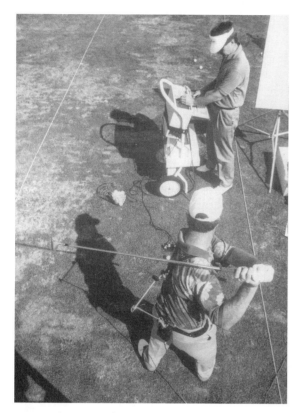

Testing the pros on the SMT helped me disprove the widely accepted fundamental of the swing: "To generate maximum power, turn your hips and shoulders to the max."

speed that allows you to maintain good balance in the body and return the clubface squarely to the ball."

A power swing is a controlled, precise swing. From address to finish, your body and club move through a series of positions. They are not difficult to attain; they don't require an unnatural degree of strength or turn; and they don't have to be performed at blinding speed. The secret to generating power in the swing is creating the proper body angles and working various parts of the body in the proper sequence. That's the only way you can arrive in the vital X-Factor backswing position, and take the X powerfully to impact.

We have already covered all of the background material you need to learn first, in order to clearly understand the more detailed swing movements I will now convey to you. Having said that, before discussing the actions of the X-Factor backswing and downswing, and showing you ways to increase your differential, it's essential that you know how to set up correctly.

Take a tip from Jack Nicklaus, surely golf's greatest player, from his book, *Golf My Way*: "If you set up correctly, there's a good chance you'll hit a reasonable shot, even if you make a mediocre swing. If you set up incorrectly, you'll hit a lousy shot even if you make the greatest swing in the world."

THE X-FACTOR SET: BODY POSITIONING

The universal fundamental is the set position at address. In this chapter I take you through the model setup position step by step. We will achieve what I call the golfer's framework. For a full driver golf swing, let's start with the feet. Spread your heels slightly wider than shoulder-width apart. A wide stance promotes a shallower swing and an elongated flat spot through the hitting area. This shallow attack track is much more powerful than a steeper angle and helps launch the ball on a more powerful trajectory.

Play the ball up (between your left instep and about an inch behind your left heel), which automatically sets your head

One of the key points to remember, when assuming the X-Factor set-up position, is to widen your stance.

behind it. This leads to impact on the upswing. Your shoulders will angle at address with the back shoulder set lower. This angle should be between 10 and 25 degrees at address, depending upon the club you are hitting. Your spine will tilt away from the target (between 2 and 10 degrees). This will feel quite level to most golfers.

In establishing perfect posture, start from a straight military stance, then bend forward from your waist (hip girdles). Your hip pockets should move out behind your heels (four to eight inches). Next, flex your knees slightly. A line down from your knees would strike the widest part of your foot. Next, tip your head and upper spine forward. Set your weight fifty-fifty (equally) over your feet. Your left foot should turn out at least 20 degrees, so it is outside your left shoulder. This important set position allows you to make a strong lateral move in the through swing. Your right foot should be turned outward less— between zero and ten degrees. If you are very flexible, it can point pretty much perpendicular to the target line (an imaginary line running from the ball to the target). These foot positions encourage a solid weight shift onto your right side and prevent you from spinning, or overturning, the hips in the backswing. Plus, they promote better rotation and a powerful move through the ball on the forward swing.

You should feel a slight degree of pressure on the inside of your legs. We pivot off the inside muscles of the legs. I also look at the angle of the legs at address. The top ball strikers have at least 5 degrees of angle on both legs, helping further to brace the body.

Set your feet, knees, hips, and shoulders square to the target line. (Some power hitters set the upper body open and the lower body closed. This promotes a wide takeaway but gives the lower body a headstart with the turn. It's a good setup to draw the ball. I do, however, caution you to avoid closing both the upper and lower body.)

The body is prepared to swing the club when you feel athletic and braced.

Remember, you will best feel balance through your feet. The feel in your feet is of weight evenly distributed from the back of the foot to the front. As I've mentioned, most great players I've interviewed nudged their weight more toward the heels. Nobody favored weight toward the toes. To balance your weight evenly—fifty-fifty between the left leg and the right leg—imagine you're standing on two separate weight scales.

Take a look at the set-up position from this unique angle to fully appreciate all its vital elements.

THE X-FACTOR BACKSWING: CREATING THE "GAP"

T hink of your takeaway action as a miniature movement to the side, rather than as rotating around the center of your body. Golfers who immediately turn in their takeaway tend to reverse pivot, shifting weight to the left (front) foot, rather than right, on the backswing.

It's important to understand that the hips make two moves: (1) lateral and (2) rotational. To properly load the right side, there must be a slight lateral move of the hips in the backswing; it keeps the right hip from reversing toward the target and is not a slide.

For the hips to rotate or turn correctly on the backswing, in a level and circular motion, there has to be some lateral movement. The concept that there is no lateral movement in the

The proper hip action is lateral and rotational.

hips, and that you should merely rotate your hips clockwise on the backswing is just absolutely wrong. It's unfortunate that I still see this written in some golf books, and still hear instructors giving students this advice, either at golf schools or at country clubs throughout America.

Hip action is tremendously important, because it allows the body's lower center to move slightly to the right, or away from the target on the backswing. When done correctly, the right side of your body will tend to line up; there will almost be a straight line, as opposed to having a "reverse C" from your right foot to your head.

For the advanced player, the arms and hands will move away in the backswing precisely with center. They are responding to center in a connected takeaway. The hands are there only for feel. The arms, hands, and club move as a reaction to the turning of your shoulders and shifting of weight. You should feel the club and arms swinging away freely, the hands and arms tension-free. Don't worry about losing control; keeping grip pressure light allows the hands to feel the clubface. Let the clubhead follow the natural shape of the swing, rising gradually along an arc; don't push it down or pick it up quickly with your hands. The club will move naturally inside the target line in response to the hands and arms. It's not your job to take the club inside; it will go inside because you are standing to the side of the ball and there is shoulder turn. Don't pull the hands and arms behind your body. Rather, keep them in sync with the center. As long as the big muscles of the upper body control the takeaway, your swing won't become quick or jerky. Keep your rhythm smooth as swing speed gradually increases. Think smooth throughout the takeaway.

As the hands reach the halfway point, you should feel that the axis of your swing has shifted to the inside of your right leg. That leg becomes the support post for the backswing, ensuring that you neither overturn the hips (and narrow your X-Factor gap), nor severely flatten the swing plane. Although I've barely mentioned the club in this book, you should understand that the clubshaft will seek the proper plane if you allow it to happen. The hands are now as far as they move away from the target, the result of moving the triangle away intact, keeping the

In the X-Factor backswing, the hands, arms, and club move as a reaction to the turning of your shoulders and shifting of weight.

As the hands reach the halfway point, you should feel the axis of the swing shift to the inside of your right leg.

One chief backswing "death move" is letting the left arm climb above the right.

wrists relaxed, and moving the club, arms, and shoulders together as a single unit: your backswing package.

Another checkpoint for this important point in the swing is the position of the right arm. It should be slightly above the left. If the right arm is visible under the left arm (viewed from the front), you have either over-rotated your forearms or center has stayed at home, and the club is too far inside the target line. From here it's very difficult to release the club, build power, and deliver the clubface squarely into the ball consistently.

As I've mentioned, when you reach the completion of the backswing, your left (front) heel can come off the ground slightly if it is pulled up as a result of the coil. Do not consciously lift the heel. This will affect your balance and lead to poor contact. Obviously your weight is over the right (back) foot. But that's not enough. It should be more toward the heel of that foot. If it goes outside the foot or toward the toes, your balance will suffer badly.

THE LETTER "L" AND ITS ROLE IN THE X-FACTOR BACKSWING

As you coil the shoulders, the arms respond. In a natural arm swing, the left arm will remain straight (connected to the upper left side of your chest) due to centrifugal force and the weight of the club. At about waist high the right elbow will naturally begin to fold. By the top of the backswing, the lower right arm and the upper right arm will form an "L," or approximately a 90-degree angle. In a model swing, the angle is 90 degrees, the perfect physics angle. Interestingly, the right elbow is around and behind the body (not to the side of the body). Many teachers think it should be pointing straight down, which is incorrect. Also, at the top of the backswing our research indicates the right forearm will be angled close to the player's spine angle. This is not exactly true with all players, but it is reasonably close (within a few degrees).

At the top of the backswing I like to see the elbows nearly

Ideally, at the top of the backswing, the upper right arm and lower right arm will form an "L."

level. Again, it's not mandatory or an exact fundamental; just a very positive position to strive for.

The second "L" is made by the right wrist. When the right wrist is fully cocked back, the angle between the right hand and wrist joint forms nearly a 90-degree angle (or L position).

The third "L" is formed by the left arm and the clubshaft at the three-quarter position in the backswing, or shortly thereafter.

These three Ls form a powerful package that will be part of your total release through the ball.

All of these angles are created by soft arms, soft wrists, and the windup of your big muscles and center. These angles will form without conscious effort on your part regarding the hands or club. They should not be forced. Rather, they should be employed by improving your free arm swing with the right elbow hinging and the right wrist hinging because of the swing action. Through practice and the knowledge of what you need to achieve, these backswing Ls can be improved by nearly every golfer. The result will be better positioning of the clubshaft and clubface and much more stored power.

At the top, your chin should have rotated away from the target. Some players turn the chin as much as 45 degrees; the average is 20 to 25 degrees. Remember, the head moves slightly. Remember, too, power hitters on the PGA Tour shift their heads back between one and four inches, some even more. Please do not forget: Trying to freeze your head in position creates tension. Tension kills speed and you might even say, it destroys the swinging action.

I would like to note several exceptions to the head movement fundamental. John Mahaffey, Colin Montgomerie, and Don Bies all tend to have the head stay in place, or perhaps even reverse slightly. All three, however, make a lateral shift of the lower body away from the target. They deviate by moving less with the upper and more with the lower. As I've mentioned, there are very few absolutes.

It's important that your left arm be firm, but not stiff. Straight, slightly bent, that doesn't matter; just don't let it tense up or become limp. There are no perfect wrist positions

A limp left arm position leads to a faulty overswing.

at the top of the swing. Having said that, if you are not a great ball striker, work on a flat left wrist (back of the wrist even with the left forearm) and a cocked right wrist. This should keep the clubface in a square power position. Many players try to gain distance by continuing to swing their hands and arms after the pivot is complete. Overswinging usually has the opposite effect. When the left arm disconnects from center, or the right elbow lifts the club, the club moves off-plane and crosses the target line on the downswing. The result is often a powerless shot or extremely inconsistent shot patterns. That said, remember even poor backswing club positions can be fixed with picture-perfect body actions to start the forward swing.

BACKSWING DRILLS: FOR CREATING THE "GAP"

DRILL 1

Set up to a ball with a driver. Next, have a friend place a club-shaft or towel on the ground, so that it extends outward from approximately your left heel, and runs perpendicular to the target line.

Now swing back a few times, trying to turn your shoulder area past the clubshaft.

The more you practice this drill, the stronger your shoulder turn will become. When you return to the course, you'll hit the ball much more powerfully.

DRILL 2

Practice your swing technique, using a wooden-handled broom. This is a drill I learned from renowned teacher Bob Toski.

Because the broom is typically longer and heavier than a standard driver, it will encourage you to turn the big muscles of your shoulders—not make an overly handsy swing.

DRILL 3

In setting up to drive, drop your right foot back twelve inches farther away from the target line than your left.

Hit a bucket of balls from this extra-closed stance, and you'll experience what it feels like to turn your shoulders powerfully on a flatter plane than your arms. Great for slicers with an overly steep shoulder tilt.

BACKSWING PROBLEMS

THE SIX DEATH MOVES IN THE BACKSWING

1. Pure Reverse Pivot
The weekend golfer has two major swing thoughts: (a) Keep the head still; and (b) turn. As a result, he or she often employs a trunk twist and a total reverse pivot.

2. Lower Body Reverse
Mr. Weekend High Handicap tries to: (a) Keep the head still; plus (b) have a weight shift. As a result, weight moves to outside of back foot, yielding an upper body counterbalance.

3. Body Sway
Often a good athlete with zero golf knowledge will employ a dramatic body sway because it feels powerful. The most noticeable fault: The head slides too far away from the target.

4. Dipping
The golfer loses his or her spine angle. The upper center drops badly and the head moves forward toward the ball. Now the only recourse is to pull away from the ball on the forward move.

5. Lifting
The golfer pulls up in the backswing. The head lifts and center raises. When the arms lift with center, the golfer is totally out of position to deliver a consistent blow.

6. Overturning (No X-Factor); Overusing the Legs
The golfer, in an attempt to gain power, turns everything (knees, hips, shoulders, and head). There is no resistance and no torque in this swing. The body action pulls the club way too far inside.

This head position is too fixed and rigid. If you keep the head locked in as you swing farther back, you'll be destined to employ golf's most common death move—the "pure reverse pivot."

SPINE ANGLE PROBLEMS

Only two things can cause your head to move up in the backswing. Either you lose your spine angle, by raising up your back/spine in the takeaway, or you lose the flex in your knees (or both).

As a result, your chin is now farther away from the ground than it was at address.

DON'T TURN IN A BARREL

The concept that there is no lateral movement in the hips and that you, as the student, should "only turn your hips" on the backswing is just absolutely wrong. I still see this written in new golf books and still hear it taught in teaching seminars.

Let me tell you what often happens if you follow this turn-in-a-barrel advice.

It is not that you do not turn the hips; you do. However, there must be a minishift in the backswing that complements the pivot action of the hips.

This is the only way you will be able to keep your right hip and right thigh area stable without reversing. It is the only way your upper right leg and right hip will occupy the same area in space.

If you only turn, your right hip will always back up, and you will be guaranteed a reverse pivot.

I believe one reason all the old-time teachers insisted on lifting the left heel in the backswing was to avoid the reverse weight shift that would naturally complement advice to turn the hips. Therefore, the additional advice of rolling off the inside of the left foot and lifting the left heel counteracted the basically incorrect advice to turn the hips in a barrel.

SHOULDER TILT AXIS (TOO STEEP/TOO FLAT)

If the shoulders tilt on a steep angle, this is a "death move." The reasons:

1. The left arm gets too vertical.
2. The body's center (and head) usually lower, or dip.
3. The clubface opens too much.
4. The swing plane is faulty; nearly vertical.

If the axis of your shoulders becomes too flat, you have also made a "death move." The reasons:

1. The left arm is too horizontal.
2. The swing becomes overly rounded.
3. The clubface closes too much.
4. The head and spine usually rise.

Pro advice: Watch yourself on video to catch this fault early, then work on these two drills.

1. If your shoulder plane is too steep, hit shots with the ball above your belt.
2. If your shoulder plane is too flat, hit balls off lies below your feet.

A Body Position You Must Avoid: The Hip Twist

This is the most common mistake that I see at our golf schools. The cause is the golfer's misconception of what he or she is attempting to do, usually based on an incorrect image of proper body movements.

Don't violently twist the hips or else you'll reduce your X-Factor gap and lose distance. Rotate them with resistence, so there's a bigger gap between your shoulders and hip turn. Remember, that's a true key to power.

To avoid backswing problems, keep this image of a balanced coiling action of the body in your mind's eye.

BACKSWING CORRECTIONS

WHEN YOU MUST THINK "SLIDE"

Normally I would never tell a golfer to consciously slide his hips or head away from the target. However, there are exceptions, and they are not all that rare.

The worst move in the takeaway and backswing action is either a lower body (lower center) or upper body (upper center) reverse. Your body weight shifts to the left side, on the backswing, instead of to your right. On the downswing, it remains on your right side, rather than shifting to your left.

To combat this serious body motion flaw, I normally have to ask the person to aggressively do the opposite—that is, consciously slide away from the target.

I might ask the student to first make a lateral move, then turn; I might ask him or her to feel weight leave the front leg early. I may even ask the student to move either the upper or lower center a foot to the side, just so I can counter the reverse move.

When students actually attempt this exaggerated move, they are always shocked when I replay it on the computer screen. They can't believe what they see. That's because what they felt they did (moved well away from the target) is usually only a fraction of what actually happens.

Sometimes we have to feel that we go a mile to move an inch, especially when we are on the golf course. Therefore, in practice I like first to see students make this move without a club. Then I give them a club without a ball. Then we hit a ball and videotape the result. Then, when they play, they can hopefully incorporate the new move into their game.

I know it will take continuous effort to produce the correct swinging action, without conscious thought. Keep working at it; the proper move will become second nature.

WHEN "TURN" IS OKAY

Many people are not extra athletic or supple. Plus, as we get older we tend to lose some stretch and rotation capability.

Whenever I face this situation on the lesson tee, I never hesitate to use the term "turn" for both the backswing and forward swing motion, including "turn the hips."

If you have difficulty making a full shoulder turn, or if you tend to slide in the backswing, try the following:

1. Think right hip back to start the backswing. This will encourage a free hip turn, which automatically increases shoulder turn.
2. Put a ball under your back foot. This will help you feel a braced leg, and stop the slide.
3. Allow your back leg to straighten (but not lock).

Remember, these measures are for special problems and can lead to reverse pivoting. Therefore, I must warn you to be very cognizant of the downside to exaggerating these stop-gap concepts.

If you tend to slide, practice turning your right hip gently clockwise.

GREAT BACKSWING IMAGES

1. Imagine your upper body fits into a tube as you bend forward. Then turn as though you were in a cylinder.
2. Imagine a needle under your chin or a sharp stick (to stay level).
3. Imagine a roof over your head (to stop raising).
4. Keep your hip pockets against a wall as you make a practice swing (to stay level).
5. Keep the right knee in cement (to stop the right knee from straightening).

THE X-FACTOR DOWNSWING: CLOSING THE "GAP"

As wide a gap as you create on the backswing, it will not amount to much unless you release the power you build up. The Power Coil and creating the perfect X won't matter unless you make the correct sequence of moves to start down.

What's the secret to a powerful downswing? It is making the correct athletic moves, and starting down with lower center or your lower body. This shift will cause your right shoulder to work downward before it moves forward (a downward rocking motion). This initial lateral motion causes other things to happen in the correct way without conscious thought on your part. When you shift lower center first and/or lower the right shoulder, the arms and hands respond in the following ways:

THE LS IN THE DOWNSWING

The three Ls you formed in the backswing will remain intact (or even increase) as you make the critical first move in the forward swing (see pages 75 and 76). This is the move that separates good ball strikers from poor ball strikers and it's done by the engine of the swing—your body—not the club, hands, or arms. The club, hands, and arms lower as the right shoulder and right elbow lower because of good body actions. As the swing continues, the left arm will fall down plane.

To keep the Ls together, you leave them alone. You do not pull down with the left arm. You do not pull the grip end of the club. Instead, you shift your lower center, or you re-center the body, which may well give you a pull feel. This can be done in several ways.

1. Shift the knees laterally.
2. Start the left knee toward the target.

The vital L positions, formed on the backswing, should be maintained as you make the critical first move in the X-Factor downswing.

3. Kick the right knee outward toward the target line (and in front of the ball).

4. Push off your right instep.

5. Bump the left hip toward the target.

6. Rock the right shoulder downward.

Do not:

1. Start with the hands (throw the clubhead from the top).

2. Rotate the shoulders (right shoulder moving out).

By simply lowering the Ls to the waist-high delivery position, you will have retained tremendous lag and saved the stored energy developed in the backswing coil described earlier.

IMPACT

When we examine the X at impact, we see that the large gap (differential) we created in the backswing is very different. At impact, the shoulders have almost caught up to the hip rotation. The gap is now much closer.

How does this happen? Does the upper body move faster? No. It moves differently, and that's the key.

Here's why: The upper body rotates around one fixed axis, the spine. The hips rotate around two axes: the right leg on the backswing, and the left leg on the downswing. The change is the result of making a lateral move toward the target. Don't think of the hips as merely turning: They shift laterally, then rotate. As Ben Hogan observed, "The lateral shift initiates the transfer of weight from right to left, and gives the upper body a chance to catch up."

All this is very nice in theory. But what does it mean to you? It means if your hips don't move laterally on the downswing, then rotate around your left leg, you won't close the gap correctly and you won't effectively use all your power.

When you start down from the top and shift weight to the left foot, the upper body tends to drop down slightly as the lower body (hip line) is poised to rise up through impact. This is natural to the athletic, side-arm throwing motion so necessary in the golf swing. As you shift and turn, the right arm and elbow should move outward a little, in front of the body. It's part of the action I referred to in *The Eight-Step Swing*, as the "sit-down" position.

The concept that you go up to the top and have your arms drop behind you is still widely accepted and taught. I've seen a lot of people try to do that. It's a terrible mistake. Again, from the top, the arms must work a little bit outward. However, this is not a move that you have time to employ consciously. If you have soft wrists, relaxed hands and arms, and employ the correct sequence of body movements, the arms will fall into the ideal hitting slot with the clubshaft falling down on a flat plane.

The last thing to move is the club. Many golfers don't understand this, and try, instead, to start the downswing by moving the club. The amateur can only see one way to get the club down and out to the golf ball and that is, quite naturally, with the hands. It is a terrible mistake. Do that and you'll unload the shaft too early and never explode through the ball. The club moves as a result of the other forces applied during the swing; it does not move on its own.

When the club reaches halfway down, with the shaft parallel to the ground, you've reached what I call the "delivery" position. I've spoken about this for many years and wrote about it in *The Eight-Step Swing*. Actually, it was Carl Welty who pointed this out to me in the late 1960s. What a fantastic discovery! At this point, it's possible to know exactly how you're going to deliver the club through impact and the ball's resulting flight. That's why I analyze this position very carefully in my teaching; you should too, with the help of videotape.

At this point in the swing, the right elbow attaches to the right side just above the hip. The left arm is virtually straight, with the upper arm hugging the chest. You're doing it right if it feels as if the arms are pulling down. (Don't consciously pull down with the hands or arms in an attempt to create the sensation.) You're re-centered and connected.

Up to this point, the clubhead should not move outside the hands. If the clubhead is outside, you have most likely consciously used your hands to release the club prematurely (using a casting action), or allowed your right shoulder to swing too far out toward the target line rather than down the imaginary plane.

Another checkpoint: If an imaginary extension of the shaft points down somewhere on or parallel to the target line, the club is on-plane and set to make solid contact. I call this an "on-line delivery." If you swing through the on-line delivery position, shifting weight from your right foot to your left foot, while clearing your hips fully around to the left, you will be hitting with maximum power.

Impact is the result of everything that happened before, but that doesn't mean you can't work on the proper impact positions. Study the photographs and text, and when you practice, freeze the key positions so you can better feel them when you swing.

Your left wrist must be flat or slightly bowed. Nothing kills power like left-wrist collapse. To promote the correct action, maintain your rotation through impact and feel, or sense, the clubhead trailing. The right wrist must be angled at impact to fit with the flat left wrist. It should look the way it does at address.

To hit powerfully accurate shots, the clubshaft must be on-line (parallel to the target line) at this point in the down-swing.

Nearly all your weight (70 to 80 percent) has transferred from your right (back) side to your left (front) leg and onto your left foot by impact. (A study by a leading golf magazine used scales to show weight shift, and showed that a lot of weight was back toward the right leg or at least centered at impact. The problem was that the study didn't use proper weight-shift gear. It actually used a needle that was moving across a dial to show weight shift. As you can imagine, the weight was moving very quickly, so the data was deemed invalid. New technology clearly shows that, in a good swing, weight shifts over to the left foot and leg through impact.)

Unlike many other instructors I talk with, I believe the right heel should also be off the ground at impact in a power swing. It is also ahead of the right toe, which indicates you pushed off

Through impact, the majority of your weight should be on your left foot and leg.

the right foot early in the downswing. This increases clubhead speed. As a matter of interest, great players and long hitters, most notably Fred Couples, John Daly, Davis Love, and Greg Norman, slide their right foot forward in the impact zone. Gene Littler, Billy Casper, and Ben Hogan did, too, during their heydays. It's scary to think how many young amateur players are not allowed to have any of this slide in their right foot, because they're told by teachers that it's a bad or faulty move. Personally, I would not take this move out of a player's swing (particularly if he or she were young) if it was used effectively to hit the ball solidly. Besides, Jack Nicklaus has his right foot slide in his downswing. (Need I say more?)

The follow-through and finish are more than just post-impact checkpoints. Striving to reach these positions will promote acceleration and keep the clubface on the ball as long as possible—two ingredients of an explosive impact. To hit through the ball fully and finish correctly, keep driving forward until you feel 99 percent of your weight has transferred to your left leg and foot. Your right shoulder should finish closer to the target than your left, and you must be in balance. Your left hip should clear fully to the left. Your right hip should have "fired" toward the target. The right toe is the only part of the right foot touching the ground.

A good test of a balanced swing is the ability to come to a full stop. In fact, many power hitters practice by swinging full out, then holding their finish like statues, completely in balance. I like this resistance concept and use it often in practice sessions with all kinds of players.

Striving to reach a full finish position will promote high clubhead acceleration at impact.

DOWNSWING DRILLS:
FOR CLOSING THE "GAP"

BASEBALL DRILL

DRILL 1

Set up normally to a teed-up ball, using a mid-iron.

Slide your left foot back toward the right, so that they practically touch each other, and the clubhead is about a foot behind the ball.

Start the backswing. When the club reaches waist level, step forward with your left foot, returning it to its original position, like a batter stepping into a pitch.

The clubhead will still be moving back as the lower body moves forward, which automatically increases wrist work and prevents the right shoulder from leading the downswing.

The Baseball Drill: After taking your normal address, slide your left foot back, next to your right, and start your backswing (left); then step forward with your left foot (right). This drill discourages an over-the-top move with the right shoulder.

DRILL 2

Practice moving the right shoulder downward at the start of the
forward swing. This trigger encourages the hips to shift laterally
toward the target. Also, it lowers the right elbow underneath
the left arm, and drops the club into the hitting slot. Now you
can hit from the inside, like all top tour players.

DRILL 3

Assume your normal address position. Then widen your stance
by placing your right foot well outside your right shoulder. Fan
the right foot outward, so it points away from you at a 45-
degree angle.

Hitting practice shots from this position helps you eliminate any upper-body slide. It maintains a wide gap between
your knees by dramatically slowing right leg action. It also
keeps you from spinning the lower body too fast.

*Hitting shots with your right foot
pointed outward 45 degrees gives you
a feeling of freedom on the backswing
(left), and keeps the lower body from
either spinning out or sliding on the
downswing (right).*

GOOD PLAYER'S DISEASE: THE DOWNSWING RIGHT SHOULDER DROP

The advanced player can get into deep trouble by overdoing the head-down, stay-behind the ball, lower-the-right-shoulder concept. It's especially prevalent in club professionals and low-handicap golfers who play poorly in tournaments. It's a terrible problem that causes an inside-out golf swing, and mishits. First, you snap hook a shot dead left, then push slice the next shot dead right. There's no way to play competitive golf with this "army golf" (left, right, left, right) shot pattern.

When the right shoulder drops excessively, the left shoulder climbs through impact. This usually causes a vertical release of the clubshaft and a topspin (hooking) action. Because the shoulders have worked too steeply, the clubshaft responds by working off-plane. The clubshaft will also be oriented on a vertical angle.

This is a clear case of the body causing the problem. Poor shoulder rotation makes it nearly impossible to swing the clubshaft on-plane. Therefore, working on your swing plane is a waste of time. You should be correcting the actions of the engine (your body).

I realize that many golfers have no idea of what an over-the-top move truly is. They believe it is the right shoulder that comes over the ball, causing a smother hook or vicious pull. In reality, it is the clubface that comes over the ball.

I demonstrate this at schools by staying super high with my right shoulder and actually spinning around when I hit the shot—I hit the shot dead straight or even push the shot with this swing.

I then ask students if I came over the shot. They say yes. I ask, "Why didn't the ball go left?" They can't answer the question.

Next, I explain rotation and clubface. I explain that when the body stops, the club and clubface can easily wrap around the body, closing the clubface badly. When they try to stop the hook, these players tend to aim farther right, grip tighter, lower the right shoulder more—exactly the wrong medicine.

CORRECT BODY ACTIONS FOR A CONTROLLED DRAW/CONTROLLED FADE

DRAW

To promote an inside-out swinging action—and controlled draw—set the body closed at address and turn the front toe in toward the target line. This will help slow your rotation through impact—a major key. Next, as you start down, slow your shoulder rotation. By slowing the body action in the forward swing, you open an inside-out attack track. Allow the arms to swing earlier and this further ensures an in-to-out path.

Remember, the keys to the draw are to set up correctly and *to slow the body action*.

FADE

To hit a guaranteed fade, open your body at address and flair your left toe out at least 20 degrees. Set your right foot closer to the target line and square off the right toe (no flair at all).

From the top of the swing, turn to the target as fast as possible. Allow the right shoulder to start out and keep it high through impact. *Rotate! Rotate! Rotate!*

Aim left, restrict your turn on the backswing, turn left, swing left, and your ball will never go left.

TOUR PLAYER ANALYSIS: PROFILE OF A LESSON PROGRAM

In June 1990, Brad Faxon came to Sleepy Hollow Country Club in Westchester County, New York, to talk with me about his golf swing. The tour stop that week was the Buick Classic, being played at Westchester Country Club, just 20 minutes down the road. This was the first time I had ever spoken to Brad, except to say hello once or twice at other tour events. Midway through our session, I shot some video of Brad swinging, then I interviewed him in depth. I wanted to know exactly what he was trying to accomplish in his golf swing. I also wanted to know the history of his game and what he felt was good and bad about it. I spent quite some time talking with Brad, also trying to give him a feel for my concepts.

At that meeting, I found out some really important points about Brad's concept of the golf swing. Frankly, I was stunned at the things he was working on. Furthermore, I told him that his ideas were opposite from mine, so he knew changes would be made if he decided to work with me. As it turned out, our work on my initial observations took two solid years, and we worked on basically the same things for three years. The following fact sheet describes our activities and Brad's progress.

WHAT I SAW ON THE VIDEO (WHAT EXACTLY WAS HE DOING?)

When I studied Brad's setup and swing in June 1990, I noticed the following faults:

1. He was too bent over at address, with his knees somewhat bowed out.
2. As he took the club away, his left arm over-extended, and his body's upper center dropped dramatically.
3. At the three-quarter point in the backswing, his thumbs

pointed almost straight up, and his left wrist was cupped. His left knee was almost "frozen." Not dynamic at all.

4. At the top of the backswing, the clubface was very open, and his left arm was disconnected from center. He had too much twist in his hips, and there was definitely evidence of a reverse weight shift.

5. He started down with the left leg sliding, the right leg staying firm. This only increased the tilt of his spine away from the target. His downswing arc was overly narrow. In fact, when I drew the narrow downswing arc on the video screen, and compared it to his wide backswing arc, the difference was huge.

6. At impact, he was in an awful position. His right foot was glued to the ground (even when hitting a driver). His head had shifted back away from the target, and his hands were too far in front of the ball. He was forced to flick his wrists at the last split second of the downswing to try to square the clubface to the ball.

7. Just past impact, the clubface had rotated into a very closed position, and the shaft came out too low, or too far left.

8. Brad's finish was long, loose, and sloppy. Even when he hit short irons, there was no end to it; no resistance.

Most of these faults were caused by poor body positioning, poor body angles, and a nonathletic sequence. It was only because of Brad's tremendous athletic prowess that he could square up the club pretty well, on most days, for most shots. However, on bad days, he would occasionally hit very weak, wild shots—well left or right of target. You can imagine how much more difficulty he had swinging this way under high-stress situations. Thankfully Brad's short game and putting game were (and still are) tremendous. Otherwise, with those bad shots sneaking into his round, he would have scored poorly, and probably lost his Tour card.

WHAT I TOLD FAXON

As always, I kept much of what I saw to myself. First, I need to know a lot more about a top player before I blurt out every swing error I observe. Second, I know there are many ways to swing a club. Plus, Brad Faxon was obviously a very confused person. As we talked I couldn't help but notice the frustration and level of anxiety he displayed. I could see his ego was very fragile at this time. I decided to give Brad a few solid ideas in an easy way. I clearly did not intend to overwhelm him with information.

He told me that the harder he worked on the things he had been told, it seemed the worse he got. He knew it was only a brilliant short game that was keeping him on the tour.

My job was to offer Brad a well-thought-out, step-by-step plan for improvement. I was honest with Brad, telling him I did see a number of things in his swing that I would like to change. I also told him I didn't agree with what he was presently working on. I warned him that we would need to dramatically change his overall thinking of body movements. Finally, I told him that the changes I would suggest would take considerable time to incorporate into his technique. In my mind I felt working on his swing had great upside potential and little downside risk.

As we walked back onto the driving range, I honestly didn't know what Brad's decision would be. I did know that his ball striking, at this time, was terrible. He knew it too. His clubface-to-ball contact was erratic. The trajectories of his shots were off.

Once on the range, I helped Brad with his setup and take-away. I also gave him a drill that would widen his downswing arc, and get him to use his right foot more actively. By then I was off to another lesson, and Brad had a major decision to make: to change or not to change his swing.

That was the beginning of our work together. Brad made the decision to overhaul his technique. I absolutely reversed everything Brad was working on, and much of everything he believed about the swing action. To do this, I showed him film of golf's greatest players and carefully explained what positive things I saw in their swings. I told him what Jackie Burke and Ken Venturi had told me about their ideas on the golf swing. He knew that these great players were both very good friends of Ben Hogan— the all-time golfing machine. I also threw in some key points that two other former top tour professionals, Claude Harmon and Gardner Dickinson, made about Hogan's swing technique. Those four men played more golf with Hogan than perhaps the rest of the world combined. (Down the road, I had Venturi speak personally to Brad, to confirm certain vital swing concepts.)

Much of my instructional message to Brad concerned body positioning, and the proper body angles he would need to achieve (or at least improve dramatically). I had to be careful as I outlined my plan. I knew I was going against everything Brad believed in the golf swing. Yet, he was ready for change. I could see in his face that he was tuned into my message. I knew he would be on the program 100 percent.

When Brad Faxon started working with me, I had to re-educate him with regard to good golf-swing technique.

WHAT BRAD WAS TRYING TO DO—RESULTS OF PREVIOUS INSTRUCTION

Brad, like many players, had been taught to keep his head down and keep his left arm straight. Further, in the five years prior to coming to me for lessons, Brad had basically worked on pulling the club down, and staying on his right leg longer. He consciously slid the left leg toward the target, while the right leg resisted releasing. In addition, Brad was trying to swing back up a vertical plane line and down on a flatter arc. These swing keys made Brad a golfer with a nonathletic look. After years of pulling the club down and sitting back on the right leg, Brad had developed a swing that had far too much lag and hang-back. Both, of course, go together.

You learn, after years of teaching, that long-term swing mistakes do not die easily. It takes tremendous effort and focus to change deeply ingrained habits. I explained to Brad that he would likely always fight these same mistakes (which tend to come back) for the rest of his life. However, at this time, we really needed to start the process, because even very minor swing changes would help him improve as a player.

THE FAXON ACTION PLAN (PART 1)

As Jackie Burke always hammered home to me: "First things first." For Brad Faxon, that meant starting to make setup improvements. First, I had Brad move his hands away from his body, and get his chest up. Previously, Brad's posture was just the opposite; hands low, upper body stooped over (which, in my opinion, is the worst starting position of all). I made this change to improve his left arm plane, round out his swing and give him a better chance to square the clubface. Second, I had Brad pinch his knees inward slightly. This was done to activate the inside muscles of the legs and establish an athletic, balanced look to his setup.

I think Brad and I talked about, or checked, his setup position virtually every time we worked together over the next two years. It is so easy to revert back to old, comfortable habits. Remember, the setup is what I call the "universal fundamental." You just can't get away with a bad setup for very long. That's why it's a good idea to constantly check your posture and all setup alignments.

The first issue we attacked in the golf swing itself was Brad's move away from the ball. We talked in detail about footwork, leg action, and turning behind the ball. To initiate the backswing, I used the word *pump* to help activate his left leg and foot. This was a term I had watched Jimmy Ballard use with many top players, and I've found it to be extremely useful myself. Pumping off the left leg into the right leg gives many students a vivid mental picture of the correct action. It tends to eliminate lifting or reversing. More important, this buzz word promotes a solid weight shift into the right foot and leg. In Brad's case, it also helped improve the early downward move of center, and that frozen right leg look.

In talking further about the takeaway, I also encouraged him to move his hands and left knee together. This trigger activated his leg and helped stop his left arm from overextending and swinging away from his body—from "disconnecting."

Brad's initial move had been to lower the head and upper torso, and to let the left arm overextend. I felt the concept of a left-side-dominated takeaway contributed to this problem. Therefore, taking a page out of Ken Venturi's lesson book, I encouraged him to use a more dominant right arm to pull center away from the target.

A couple of other key things that helped Brad iron out some of his problems were swinging with a glove under his left arm and copying Paul Azinger's and Billy Mayfair's exaggerated upper-body move in the takeaway. To a degree, I did begin to see improvement through 1990. Still, we both knew how much work remained.

THE FAXON ACTION PLAN (PART 2)

During a conversation with Brad one night at my house early in 1991, he indicated he was discouraged and wondered if he could make the more serious swing changes so necessary to improve his ball striking. I told Brad he must remain patient, and that improving swing technique was only one part of becoming a top player. I then reviewed some of the goals we had mutually discussed. I took each one and broke it down to the lowest common denominator. All of a sudden things didn't appear so daunting. Each point seemed very achievable once we got down to working on a few simple moves. I went over a drill for each of the areas we were trying to improve. This is a procedure I've repeated numerous times with hundreds of students. I call it *getting on with achievable things*. It is not doing everything at once. It is doing simple drills that isolate specific areas of the golf swing. Here's what we worked on:

Split Grip Drill

I had Brad hit shots with his hands approximately six inches apart on the club's handle. This drill allowed him to hit the ball almost entirely with leg pump, body shift, and body rotation.

Stake Drill

I put a stake in the ground, to the left of the target line, and a few feet in front of the ball. I wouldn't allow Brad to pull the club to the left after impact, which is where it tended to go. This drill, more than any other, helped Brad use his big muscles (not his hands) to create width in his downswing. He also learned to square the club with center.

Sidehill Lie Drill

I had Brad hit shots with the ball positioned above his feet. This baseball-swing-style action helped flatten or round out his upright backswing.

Upper Body Drill

I had Brad hit balls trying to get out in front of the shot prior to impact. Brad felt his upper body drifting well past the ball, only it didn't happen. It was almost impossible for Brad to overdo this drill. I also had Brad look to the target absolutely as fast as he could. This began to synchronize his arms to his center.

Moe Norman Drill

To counteract the drop of center in Brad's takeaway, I had him set up like Moe Norman, the eccentric but talented Canadian pro: extra-wide stance, club twelve inches behind the ball. The results were immediately positive.

The wide stance lowered Brad's center of gravity. It also made it easier for him to stay level in the takeaway, and stay behind the ball. Starting the club a foot behind the ball elimi-

Starting the club approximately twelve inches behind the ball, like Moe Norman at address, then swinging, eliminated Brad's left arm "run off"— one of his greatest problems.

nated the left arm "runoff." I always hoped Brad would actually try this unorthodox setup in a tournament, but it was just too radical. Still, this drill helped a lot.

THE FAXON ACTION PLAN (PART 3)

In early 1992, I convinced Brad to stick with a steel shaft. However, one of the best things I did for Brad (with respect to equipment changes) was to suggest a shorter driver with more loft, a tip I learned from Bruce Lietzke, one of golf's greatest tee-ball players. Around this time, after a heck of a lot of hard work, Brad's game was showing very good progress. Although

NOTE: *Brad pulled it together in 1990, winning $230,000, and then, in 1991, he won the Buick Open. Faxon also won $422,088, to finish 34th on the PGA Tour money list.*

his tour statistics did not indicate a huge change, anyone playing with Brad could see his bad shots were not nearly as bad. And, of course, Brad still possessed exceptional short game skills. He also had some great periods of ball striking. I still saw Brad often, but not quite as much as 1991, when we either talked or worked together virtually every week.

I was with Brad all week at the 1992 Tournament of Champions where he lost in a playoff to Steve Elkington. We worked hard again in Palm Springs at the Bob Hope, and then more in Florida. I was at the Masters, the U.S. Open, and the PGA working with Brad. At the PGA, held that year at Bellerive in St. Louis, I saw Faxon's game reach a new level. I walked around eighteen holes with Bob Rotella, Brad's longtime friend and sports psychologist. Both Bob and I watched Faxon hit every type of shot on call. It was beautiful to see. Later that year at the Tour Championship held at Pinehurst, I saw the same thing. It was no surprise to me that, in 1992, Brad won two PGA Tour events (New England Classic; International), and lost two others in playoffs. He finished the year 8th on the money list, winning $812,093.

One of the last times I really worked with Brad Faxon occurred in Jamaica at the end of 1992. A year before, he had seemed out of place at the World Championship, but this year he was a different person. Full of confidence, he was able to play the super tight Tryall Golf Course well, finishing 7th there to cap off a tremendous season.

As I left Tryall, I reviewed Brad's year. Had Brad won those two playoffs, I thought, he might have been the Tour's 1992 Player of the Year.

As the plane left the runway, I knew it was an awesome year, and very close to a monster year. Faxon was poised for even bigger and better things.

Since that time, Brad has performed very well. I think there are a lot more wins in Brad—even a major championship, or two.

The new and improved Faxon action.

FINAL REVIEW:
LOAD, UNLOAD, EXPLODE

Here is a final checklist of the basic idea I've presented in this book.

- Work to achieve the athletic set positions at address.
- Think of your body as two halves. Coil the upper half over a braced lower body.
- LOAD power and weight onto your right leg, or backswing pivot point. Build a power coil.
- Feel resistance on the insides of both legs.
- Think of your body as the engine of the swing; it winds and shifts in a small space.
- There must be coordinated motion and rhythm to produce powerfully accurate shots.
- The arms attach to the engine. The arms work with the engine. The arms and body synchronize—they work together. The arms stay basically in front of your body centers.
- Learn the Shift-Rotate-Throw downswing sequence. That's how you UNLOAD power. Remember, you do this in all other sports; you can do it in golf!
- Swing in balance.
- Let the arms operate on automatic pilot, returning the club to the ball at speeds of around 100 miles per hour. That's how you EXPLODE power.
- Remember that every action causes a reaction. Make the initial actions correct, and the following actions will be correct as well.

Look at golf in a way that relates closely to other sport activities. If you think of golf as being different from all other sports or throwing actions, you will make golf far more difficult than it needs to be. Instead, learn the athletic golfer set position and then the fundamental body positions. By doing so, you will be able to swing the golf club easier and with far more power.

I feel that absolutely nothing is more important than learning to swing the club. Creating that beautiful swinging action is a major goal. I know that proper body setup, body angles, and correct sequencing will allow you to swing the club with much more force and, furthermore, without expending excessive energy.

I wish you well in your quest for golf excellence and hope that the information in this book helps you to reach your golfing potential.